If I Won 25 Million Dollars In The Lottery

✦

A Book about Money, Hope, and Happiness

Larry Steinhouse

iUniverse, Inc.
New York   Bloomington

If I Won 25 Million Dollars in the Lottery
A Book about Money, Hope, and Happiness

Copyright © 2010 Larry Steinhouse

iUniverse books may be ordered through booksellers or by contacting:

iUniverse
1663 Liberty Drive
Bloomington, IN 47403
www.iuniverse.com
1-800-Authors (1-800-288-4677)

ISBN: 978-1-4401-9872-4 (pbk)
ISBN: 978-1-4401-9874-8 (cloth)
ISBN: 978-1-4401-9873-1 (ebk)

Library of Congress Control Number: 2009913499

Printed in the United States of America

iUniverse rev. date: 01/06/2010

If I Won 25 Million Dollars In The Lottery

I dedicate this book to My Love, Carol, who believes in me.

Foreword

I told my father that I was writing a book. He then asked, "So what's it about?"

I answered, "Money."

He responded sarcastically, "Just what the world needs, another book about money!"

I have read several books on money and motivation. These are subjects that I am fascinated with. I love the stories told by the rich about how they became rich. It is often the same story. It begins in a poor neighborhood with parents that had migrated here from another country, or maybe they were thrown out of their country. They never spoke English when they arrived and maybe they raised chickens to feed the family. Sometimes the stories are those of orphans, but most of the stories start out being told by a now very wealthy person who once was very poor.

This isn't one of those books. It is quite possible that most of you, reading this book, have more of a net worth than I did when I started writing this book. Even as I finish this book, I would imagine that you still may have more.

That is why I am writing this book. I am here with you! I lost it *all* and I need to start from scratch. I have not reached my newfound wealth; in fact I am far from it. So as you read this book and enter this journey, you should know that I am here with you. I have made many of the mistakes you have made or are going to make and I have learned from them. The principles and ideas in this book have come from those lessons, as well as the observations and research of successful people. This book will help guide you and help keep you on the right track.

I believe that you and I will reach our goals and desires. This book is an instruction manual on how to do just that. Like other instruction manuals, you may want to skip some steps or pick and choose which you would like to use. I truly believe that if you follow this book you will have all that you desire!

A few suggestions for you as you read this book:

Have a pencil or pen and a pad of paper handy to take notes and write down some of the important parts of the books for quick reference. Maybe you should put page numbers next to the notes as well. I also suggest that you do the exercises in the book. The book can surely be read without doing the exercises but, if you do the exercises, you will be able to get the full benefit of the book and the ideas expressed.

Finally, I suggest that you reread the book several times. Read it at least three times in the first year of your journey. I have found that with every self-help book that I read I always find something I missed in each rereading of the book.

You should also know that this book is timeless. It is written at the time of the great recession of 2009, but the ideas and principles of this book should be on everyone's minds always.

Thank you for reading my book and enjoy the journey to your newfound Money, Hope and Happiness-- and maybe $25,000,000 from the lottery, as well.

Larry Steinhouse
Author

Table of Contents

Chapter 1

Where Are We?

It is the year 2009 and it is a good time to be broke! Why, you ask? Because everyone is broke, or in fear of being broke. The heyday of the late nineties and the easy money-lending of the 2000s made it easy for too many people to spend or invest borrowed money. Let's take a bit of a time shift and later I will explain again why it is a good time to be broke.

I remember hearing a story, a long time ago, that may even be an urban legend. This is how I recall it. William Rockefeller, easily one of the richest men alive in the late 1920's, was said to be getting a shoe shine at a shoe shine stand. He over-heard the man shining his shoes bragging about how he (the shoe shiner) was going to be rich because he found "the secret" to investing in the stock market. As the story continued, Rockefeller immediately went to his office and sold all of his stocks. The stock market crashed and the Great Depression happened soon thereafter. Of course, Rockefeller retained his riches because he sold all of his stocks. He took the sign of the shoe shiner's enthusiasm as a clear warning that the stock market was no longer the place to invest.

Let me explain.

You see, as Warren Buffett puts it, "be fearful when others are greedy." If that story was non-fiction, then it is easy to understand that Rockefeller was very fearful. After all, if a common shoe shiner could brag about the riches he could make in the stock market, then how could the highly educated and learned people like Rockefeller be smarter or richer than a common shoe shiner? Not that there aren't stories about people pulling themselves up in society, but this clearly was not going to be one of them.

The Great Depression happened simply because the value of anything material has a current value. With time, the right effort, and, most importantly, demand for an object, anything should increase in value. Unfortunately, when the demand for an object is artificially inflated, the price of the asset also becomes artificially inflated. This creates artificial wealth and, most importantly, the greed factor!

The greed factor is simply the notion, "If he could do it, so could I." So if your neighbor has come over one day to tell you of the brilliant stock pick he made at $7/share and it is now $107/share, you decide you can do this as well. After all, he is of the same education and social status as you, so you must be as smart as he. Of course he neglected to tell you of the last ten poor stocks he invested in and that he is still down thousands for the year. All you know about is the mega gain, so you try it! Of course the stock you buy at $35 a share, expecting to go to $350 a share, goes down to $20 and you are extremely disappointed. I know this because it has happened to me several times.

You don't lick your wounds and give up; you continue to try to make it rich in the stock market because you continue to replay in your mind your neighbor's joy in telling you that story of his making all that money, even though you have little to no knowledge of the stock market and why a stock goes up or down.

Now you think about the equity you have in your biggest asset: *your home*. Interest rates are down, so you borrow the money and invest in stocks and real estate. As the common man, why wouldn't you do this? After all, you could borrow the money at about 5% per year interest while most stocks appeared to be going up over 35% per year, for a net profit of about 30%! Some stocks were going up over 100% per month and if you picked one of these, well that could be a lottery winner right there!

I wonder how many people reading this are laughing at themselves, for they have thought this very thought and borrowed money from all kinds of sources—like equity loans, or credit cards, or other sources like 401K withdrawals or even credit card advances—just to pay the "ticket" to ride the "gravy train" of future wealth.

Think about the possibilities. You could start with a small amount of capital, let's say $1000, pick the right stock or stocks and your money could double every month. If my math is correct, that would be over 2 million dollars by the end of the year. Isn't this what we expect when we go into the stock market?

Jealousy, and the idea that "this is America, the land of opportunity," makes the common man do very stupid things with his money. The Depression was said to happen because too many people borrowed money on margin to buy stocks. The demand for stocks stopped because people could not borrow any more money. This made the demand for stocks decrease and the stock prices started to fall, triggering a downward spiral of stock prices.

Simply put, you had the stock holders watching the stock prices go down and selling stocks, which of course lowered the price of the stock, which of course made more stock holders sell, which lowered the stock price more, which of course caused more people to sell, which of course…

…I think you get the point.

Unfortunately, there was another problem: leverage. Leverage is when you use other people's money to invest in or buy something. Leverage is an investor's dream! It is simply borrowing or using money that is not yours. You will pay a fee for that money, usually interest or maybe an upfront fee. You then purchase your investment asset, sometimes using that very asset as collateral for that loan.

So in the Roaring Twenties (that's the 1920's for those who are too young to have heard that expression), many people borrowed money to invest in the stock market. As the stock prices started to fall at the end of the 20's, the "lenders" started to demand their money back. Now the investors had to sell whatever stocks they had to try to repay these loans. Well here comes another selling frenzy, causing the stocks to dive further in price.

Now we have several banks and investment houses out thousands of dollars that they lent to the "shoe shiners" and other average people with no chance of ever recovering this money. This caused banks to literally close their doors and everything from small life savings to fortunes were lost by millions of people and corporations. Even the people who were responsible with money lost everything they had because the banks were irresponsible with the assets of these depositors.

Next, the corporations who lost millions because the stock price tanked had to do something to increase profits, so they simply "cut the fat." They laid off thousands and thousands of people. Now millions were out of work, leading to less money flowing into the economy, lowering sales estimates for many companies, causing demand for everything to go down, causing prices to go down, causing more losses, causing more fat to be cut and the vicious cycle continued until there was a recession and then a depression! A depression, as it is defined, is a severe economic downturn that lasts several years.

In July 1929 the Dow Jones industrial average closed just at the peak of about 347.47 dollars. Then it all came to an end. In December 1932 it was about 59 dollars. That is about an 84% loss in value. Imagine that! That means, in today's economy, the stock market which peaked in 2007 at about 14,000 dollars would be at about 2,100 dollars. Perish the thought! Unemployment was about 25% and welfare consisted of soup lines to feed the poor and homeless. Tent cities were where many of these people would live.

Now you start to think about what you have just read and you begin to realize that I was talking about the Great Depression of the 1930's, but this sounds so familiar. That is because it is happening again. Think about it; the banks, in the 10-year period of 1997 to 2007, went on a lending frenzy. To qualify for a loan you simply needed to pass the mirror test. If you could *fog* a mirror, you qualified for a loan. Having sold real estate in this time I was privy to some strange loans. I was told by lenders that I didn't have to ask what the income of the buyer was as long as the buyer had a decent credit score. Sometimes they could even overlook the credit score as well.

I was literally able to help people buy homes or investment properties even if they had no income. I was amazed and went with the flow. Now we are all experiencing the results of those bad loans and easy underwriting guidelines.

Money can be described as a bowl of candy. Did you ever notice that when a candy bowl is full, people will take huge handfuls, but as the bowl starts to get empty, people become picky as to which piece they want? They take less as the bowl empties until there is but one piece left that is stale and old; but it still gets eaten after it is rejected several times.

When money is flowing, people just start taking it. When banks will lend you money without thinking of whether you will be able to repay it, people will line up in droves to get their share of the easy money. Hundreds, thousands, millions, whatever the bank will give them, they will take for any reason at all.

They don't even think about how much they are taking, they just take. If the bank will lend homeowners 125% or more of the value of a home, they take it. Why not? The home values are going up 30% a year, making this low risk for the bank and the borrower. Of course the borrower can't default because after all it is his or her home and no one would risk losing a home to foreclosure, right? At least that is the theory.

Now, like in the 1930's stock market crash, people start to try and sell their homes and try to keep whatever profit they have. Of course the banks have started to tighten lending requirements and loans are harder to get, making the buying pool smaller, causing supply to be high. Now, the basic supply and demand principals come into play. With less people able to qualify for loans, the demand continues to lower and the supply continues to increase.

If you have ever shopped for a car and wanted to trade in your current car, you may have heard of the expression "upside down." This is when you owe more on your car than it is worth. This is not so terrible when your car is worth $10,000 and you owe $11,000. Actually the dealer will probably just "roll" the $1000 difference into your new loan, or you will find the thousand dollars in your savings account to make up the difference, allowing you to purchase the new car.

Now take that same scenario and imagine the car is worth $10,000 but you owe $25,000. You then come to find that the dealer you bought the car from a year ago didn't tell you that it was only worth $12,000 when you bought it. What would you do?

You would probably stop paying on the loan and let the bank inherit your problem. After all they played a part in it also, by not truly evaluating the cost of the car and giving you a loan for an overpriced car.

Now think about this. If you had a home in today's market that was worth $350,000 and you owed $500,000 on that home, because the market has plummeted as it has, should you keep it or let the bank foreclose on the home? The answer is complicated and simple at the same time. The real risk and fear is ruining your precious credit rating. How much will your credit rating really affect you in the future? You need to realize that you can still get car loans and credit cards but at a higher interest. You then need to calculate how much money that difference will really cost you. Is it worth it to try to wait out the market for the home to be worth your loan? Or should you temporarily destroy your credit rating and let the bank inherit your upside down equity problem? All this will truly cost is additional interest on whatever you would like to buy in the future. I will not give you my opinion on this at this time but it a serious thought to be had by many with this problem.

Other people have the problem of the increasing loan payment. Many people in this situation simply cannot afford the new payments so they simply have no choice but to stop paying and let the banks foreclose.

Now the foreclosures start bringing even more supply into the market and then prices continue to spiral down. The great housing recession/depression begins.

The banking industry goes into a downward spiral and the rest of the economy goes along for the freefall along with it. Everything suffers. Most consumers not only do not have the money to spend, but those who do are scared to part with it.

Almost everyone in this type of economy has the fear of poverty. Poverty becomes the thought of the day, the month, or the year for each and every person living in this type of economic environment. Every penny becomes valuable to everyone. The same people who, years before, dipped into the candy bowl full of money are now looking for those scraps and crumbs at the bottom of the dish. Unfortunately, there just aren't enough scraps to find.

So now what?

Well, as I write this, our newest President, Barack Obama, is faced with what is probably the toughest economy and some of the toughest financial quandaries of all time. He has signed bill after bill that is designed to keep companies like GM or Citicorp from failing. He has also signed other bills that will keep the average homeowner in their homes and avoid foreclosure.

Why is he doing this? Well in our minds, it is simply to avoid the inevitable: the next Great Depression. If foreclosures continue, then the price of houses will continue to fall, causing more houses to go into foreclosure, causing more prices to fall, causing more foreclosures, etc, etc. Sound familiar? It sounds a lot like the 1930's all over again.

At the time of writing this, the stock market is a little, very little, over half of its peak of about $14,000 and struggling to stay in the $7500 range. This brings more fear to just about everyone living in this economy.

You are almost at the end of this chapter and you are wondering why this book is so gloomy. As the reader you are probably asking yourself, "Why am I reading about these things that are making me even more fearful of the times?"

It is important to understand that fear is an opportunity. This is one of the lessons that will be the most important for the reader of this book to remember.

I will repeat it again: with fear comes opportunity. This is often repeated by the great Warren Buffett who, as I understand it, took that mantra from one of his mentors.

So what does this mantra mean to you? Well first I want to tell you about my karate days. I am not very athletic nor very graceful, I would consider myself the average student and I actually never did get my black belt. I tell you this because I want you to understand that the analogy I am going to make is as average as both of us.

When I was in karate class, we started to learn to spar. This is fighting for the layman. In sparring we would punch and kick each other as if we were on the street and in a real fight. I do have to admit that we were wearing padding and hitting each other with less intensity than if it were to save our lives in the street, but nevertheless I was scared. At times I would even skip or hop back so as to avoid getting hit. Or at least try to avoid getting hit.

Something that I learned, after being bruised several times, was that if I moved back, a few things happened. First, you can't throw a powerful kick or punch when you are moving backward. Think about it, you are moving away from your target. The next thing I learned was that as I moved back, I actually moved into my opponent's power range. This simply meant that his arm or leg would be almost fully extended when it hit me. This would make his punch more powerful and more effective.

The fear of the pain this caused would, of course, make me try to move back more, making more of his punches more powerful, giving me more pain, making me more fearful… well, you get the point.

One day I realized something that made all of the difference. I stopped moving back. In fact, I started moving forward. This was great! The punches I was receiving were less powerful and my punches would connect now. Then finally my opponent was actually the one who started moving back.

You see, when I was fearful, my opponent got greedy and took advantage of the situation. When I started to adapt and stopped allowing myself to be afraid, I was able to take advantage of my opponent's weakness—which was, simply, fear. When his fear increased, I got greedy and started to win.

The world is very fearful right now. You should be thinking of all of the ways to get greedy. Don't move backwards, move forwards. This is not only good for your financial situation; it is good for your mind.

Millions of us are so afraid of not having a job, or of the stock market crashing, or that we will simply not be able to pay our bills, that we have become all-consumed by fear and we forget the basics.

Lack of discretion and over-confidence is what put the world in this economic mess. I promise you that over-caution will keep you here, in this mess. It is important to realize that over-caution is just as bad as over-confidence.

Why do most people buy houses and invest in stocks when prices are high, but when prices are low and a real bargain, they move back? It makes no logical sense! In this economy, as an average person, like me, we should be very excited. This is the economy that will bring out the next unknown millionaires, or even billionaires.

"Necessity is the mother of invention," we are told. In an economy like this one, a major recession or a depression, new ideas will be formed out of the necessity of this economy. Ideas to help people will form the most quickly. Institutes for learning new skills for the unemployed that will be co-sponsored by the government are just one of the many ideas that will set the course of the future of the country, or even the world.

Ideas on new products and services will form in this economy. As the next ten years unfold, companies that were just ideas formed in the minds of people just like you and I, discussed over the kitchen table, like Kinko's or Rita's Water Ice or Starbucks, ideas as simple as the Frisbee or the Hoolahoop will be invented by people who move forward and face and embrace the fear.

If your mind has not been thinking of the many ways you and people just like you can take advantage of the fear and move forward, then you will miss the next great economy that will follow this recession/depression.

I started off by saying how this is a good time to be broke, because everyone else is. Now let me explain.   Everyone you talk to has a story about how they lost money. They either tell about the stock market losses, a real estate loss, or losses on their 401k plan.   I hear the same joke over and over about people calling their 401k plans a 201k because they lost about half of what was in the plan.

So why am I so excited? I am excited because I am not fearful. I will face the fear head-on. I am going to move forward. People like you and I are now on an even playing field. Everyone is now suffering financially. It is time for a revolution, for the fearful to stop being fearful and be smart.

Do you remember when you were a child and you were playing ball? Invariably you or someone else hit the ball way off to the right or left and demanded a *do-over*. How about the last golf game you played: do you recall someone hitting a stray ball and asking for a *mulligan*?

Well, here it is: your do-over, your mulligan. You have a chance to start all over. You can ride the real estate market up or ride the stock market again. You can look for that opportunity to invent a new product or service or simply improve on a product or service.

The next financial wave is coming; are you going to ride the wave or hide at the top of the safe sand dune and not get wet? You seriously need to decide this now, because this type of opportunity comes but once in a lifetime and the last one happened 80 years ago.

So as you read further into this book, you will discover things about yourself that will make this journey exciting, fun, and rewarding—and not just rewarding financially, but mentally as well.   You will discover the rules of both money and happiness. You discover your dreams and desires and ways that you can reach them. You discover some of the things that have held you back from your successes and how to overcome these challenges. You will discover how to live a better life and break away from this recession. You will learn to move forward and avoid any future recessions. You may even discover your true meaning of life.

Oh, I forgot that this book has something to do with winning the lottery. We will get to that in future chapters, but right now I want you to do me a favor and read my first set of Powerball numbers out loud. I will explain this as we go on.

Remember, read them out loud!

15 27 30 32 53 Powerball 11

Chapter 2

"Money Makes The World Go Around"

It is amazing to me that something as important as money is so misunderstood. Money is simply pieces of paper or trinket-size coins that we exchange for goods and wares. Sounds simple, doesn't it? Well as you have already surmised, it is not simple at all.

There was a time when money was equal to a value of gold. Simply put, your certificate, or dollar, was equal to a specific amount of gold. That would mean that when you acquired money, it was simply "holding" the receipt for the piece of gold held in a safe place like the Federal Reserve. While you held that dollar or "gold certificate," you laid claim to or "owned" that piece of gold. Of course coins such as nickels, dimes and quarters could lay claim to their equivalent to a piece of gold as well.

There was a base amount of gold that the amount of money in "the streets" was equivalent to. Of course that would operate on the assumption that everyone in the gold reserve was honest, but assuming that were the case, for every piece of gold in the reserve, an amount of gold notes or dollars would circulate among the people. The notes were more reliable and trustworthy forms of payment.

This is simple to understand, because if gold were valued by weight, then on which scale should or would it be measured? If you went into a car dealer to buy a $30,000 car, then you would need about 2 pounds of gold (assuming gold was worth about $900/ounce in today's market). If your scale said it was 2 pounds and the dealer's scale said it was 1.93 pounds... well, you can quickly understand the problems with this scenario. So the dollar is more reliable and much more convenient. Also, can you imagine having to carry those 2 pounds of gold in your pocket?

Now it is important to understand that the gold standard kept all money equal in basis around the world. Everyone, using the gold standard, would know exactly how much gold they could lay claim to by a standard conversion figure. This conversion would be the amount of gold that it was equivalent to. We here in the United States converted it into dollars while other countries called the notes different things, like marks or pounds or francs, but it all meant the same thing, an equivalent amount of gold held by the various governments.

I am not trying to bore you with the unimportant details of money, but like every troubled child, money had troubled beginnings.

So what happened to the gold standard?

Remember the Great Depression? (It's in the first chapter if you forgot.) In 1933, the height of the Great Depression, a new president, Franklin Roosevelt, made a drastic decision to go off of the gold standard. Money was simply "printed" and basically infused into the economy. It had what I can only understand as a mystery value. It started with deflating the dollar or basically splitting the dollar into lower worth than its equivalent amount of gold, but it is unclear to me its true conversion at this time.

Gold would still have a value but it would no longer be a standard. In fact sometimes a dollar is worth more than its gold equivalent and other times it is less. Gold is simply a commodity like other collectables. So where does that leave money?

Well, here it is: money is a piece of paper—or in the case of coins, a hunk of metal—that is WORTHLESS! Imagine taking a piece of paper with your picture on it and going to the grocery store and trying to redeem it for a loaf of bread? You would be thrown out immediately, but put a dead president on it and well, you would get some respect!

Now I make this point because that is the problem with the way people treat money. They simply have no respect for it. They throw it away like toilet paper in the wind, a new oversized house, a new oversized TV, a new oversized car and so on and so on.

If we exchanged real gold for our possessions we might feel the impact of our purchase. Imagine again plopping down 2 real pounds of gold to buy a car. Then maybe the impact of our purchase would be understood each time we purchased something.

Now, I am truly a big fan of money and it is my goal to accumulate and circulate as much money as I can. So where does that lead us?

I remember reading a self-help book once that said something about paying attention to clichés. At first I thought about racist and rather insulting clichés and made the decision that following clichés was bad advice. As time went by, I noticed something interesting about the clichés with regards to money. I noticed that they relate well to money and should be pondered with respect. I have chosen a few money clichés to make a standard of rules to follow, using the cliché as a basis of the rule.

In this chapter I will go over the positive, "must follow" clichés, and in the next chapter, I will discuss the negative and "why not to follow" clichés about money.

As someone who has let money slip through my fingers several times, I truly believe these are the rules of money you should follow every day. It is important for the reader of these rules to understand that it is not my intention to explain the true meaning or origin of these clichés, but rather to use them as a list of rules to give money the respect it deserves.

So let's begin….

Believe it or not, these are just some of the hundreds of clichés I found regarding money. Google is a great tool for research!

RULE 1
"Another day, another dollar."

This is by far most the important rule you can have for money. You must earn money (a dollar) every day! In these trying times so many Americans are losing jobs. This is an awful feeling and I know firsthand how terrible this can be, for the person who lost the job and for his or her family as well. I know because it has happened to me. I remember the long walk to the train station only an hour after I had arrived to my office to find, to my surprise, my boss waiting for me so that he could tell me this was my last day.

I felt outright shame walking to the train, going home to my wife at the time to tell her I was unemployed and scared. I have to admit there was nothing she could do or say that would make me feel better. So what did I do? I followed this rule.

I took my day, actually the next two days, to lick my wounds. Then I immediately started to call companies in the same business as the company I worked for. I also called recruiting agencies to find work. I simply made it my job to find a job.

The problem with many who are out of work today is that they do not follow this rule. If you are not working, you are not bringing in any dollars. Sounds simple, doesn't it? Well this is a rut that people fall into. They believe that they are entitled to the amount of money they made with their previous employer, so they demand that amount of their next employer. Some even have the audacity to ask for more!

I truly understand the statement "but that is what I need to live," but that statement is ridiculous! If you are unemployed and making nothing, how are you living now?

Go out and make a dollar today! Find work somewhere, but find it. It is okay to search for another job while you are working a low-paying temporary job. As a matter of fact, I insist on it!

Think of it this way: if your employer did not fire you or close the company or cut your department and instead said, "To save money and keep the doors open, as of the next pay cycle all salaries will be cut in half," what would you have done? You certainly would be angry or at least be disappointed, but if unemployment was high and the prospect of finding a new job within two weeks proved to be difficult, would you stay or quit? If you quit you earn nothing. If you stay, you earn half and have the opportunity to follow this rule and also to find another job.

My point is simple: if you are suddenly out of work and have the opportunity to earn something while you look, then do it! You don't have to be a psychologist to understand that someone out of work will quickly fall into a depressed state and become, in their own mind, more and more worthless. Even if you truly cannot find work somewhere, volunteer to do something for someone or some organization to feel a sense of self-worth. But always remember that you must make that buck today and every day. This will get you refocused and employed quickly.

When I was out of work it only took me 5 weeks to get back into a position that was similar to the one I was in. Of course, I was on mostly commission, so my pay rate was substantially lower, but I pressed on to make my buck for the next day.

Simply put, if you have to push aside your pride and earn something, anything, do it today. Don't wait!

RULE 2
"Time is money."

There are 2 significant parts to this rule that must be followed.

1) Time can be translated into its hourly equivalent. Simply put, it is like an hourly wage. As an exercise you should determine what your hourly worth is. Some people make money on an hourly basis and it makes sense to just use that figure. For example, if you are working at a grocery store and your hourly wage is $12/hour, then that is a good figure to use for your current hourly worth.

I want to be clear here in that I point out the word "current" in the last sentence. Your actual hourly worth may be more or less than your current hourly worth for that grocery store. You may have a second job, for example, that nets you $9/hour, so you should average the rates. You may have overtime pay that brings you extra pay, such as time and a half pay for the hours over 40 per week, and again you should average in this rate. You may also just be at that grocery store awaiting a better rate of pay from another employer, making this hourly number temporarily smaller than it will be in the future. Nevertheless, determine a rate for which you are currently working and know that rate at all times.

For those on salary or fixed wages you must, for the purpose of this exercise, convert your annual rate to an hourly rate. To do this, simply divide the number of actual annual working hours that you normally work into your salary. For example: if you work an average of 45 hours per week and 52 weeks per year, then your average working hours for the year is 2350 hours (45 hours per week x 52 working weeks). Now take your salary—let's use $40,000—and divide it by the hours. That will be ($40,000/2340) and you get about $17/hour. I would bet that most salaried people have never really thought about the hourly wages they make, and that has been a big mistake.

If you are a commission salesperson or work with bonuses, simply take your expected commission or bonus for the year and use the same division.

Remember: time is money, so if your hourly wage is unknown then how do you know how much money you could make if you worked a few hours more? Let's say you wanted a new car and the new payment was $150 more than your old payment. If you needed the extra, could you work about 9 hours more a month to afford it?

Of course, a better question is whether or not the extra time is worth the advantages of the new car. This is also where the actual amount of your hourly wage is important. You should be able to convert your bills into an hourly cost, not a monetary cost. Think about this conversion very carefully with everything you purchase and your life will change.

For example, imagine your boss said to you, "James, I need you work 20 more hours a month for the next 5 years, about 4.5 extra hours a week, and for this work I will give you, as compensation, a new car." If your car had just died, or were about to, would you take it? You need the car, can do you the hours for the next 5 years?

Now think about this. The average car payment for an average car is about $340/month for 5 years. That means, if you make $40,000/year, you are currently working 20 hours a month, or half a work week each month, to pay for your car.

Remember earlier when I discussed the value of that piece of paper we call the dollar? I stated it was worthless. Well we both know that it isn't worthless, but we treat it that way all the time.

Forget the gold standards and all that history of money and instead convert money into time. Your time! You should ask yourself, how many hours of work does that item cost, not how many dollars is it. I tell you now that when you start to think this way your entire outlook will change.

Here is an example to think about: let's say you decide to take the day off and play golf because you found out the local golf club is having a half-day special, and you can save today if you play today. Normally the golf at this exclusive club is $60 to play, but today it is $30. Wow, a big $30 savings! Let's examine the cost of this day.

If, by the example above, you are making $17/hour and work an average of 9 hours a day, then for that day you lost $153 in wages. You saved $30 on the golf outing, but it still cost you $30 to play. That makes the total golf outing cost equal $183. Now think about this: it will take you almost 11 hours of work to make back the money for that day. Of course that does not take into account the other incidentals such as lunch, drinks, or balls lost; it may be another 2 or 3 hours to make that up as well.

How about that big screen HDTV? About 147 hours of work for the $2500 TV. That is almost a full month's pay!

You should clearly think about each and every purchase this way. How many hours will it take to buy that item, not how many dollars does it cost. The monetary experts talk about the dollar as its buying power compared to each country. They compare how much a US dollar will buy compared to that country's currency. If you understand this, then you understand that each and every person or family has their own micro economy within their own household as it relates to hours worked.

The cost of an item is fixed for both the high earner as well as the low earners. If a car costs $30,000, it costs that much to someone who makes $25/hour or someone who makes $17/hour. The amount of hours each of these people has to work for that car is what changes, not the price. Compare the cost to your internal economy, not the world's external economy.

So what does this mean? To alter another great cliché, "Don't spend the dime if you can't do the time!"

2) The second significance of "time is money" is that money, if it is properly nurtured in an investment, will also produce money over time. Time after time we are told about the compound features of money, but most do not fully understand the impact of this.

One of my heroes, PT Barnum, used to say about money something that went like this: "People can't work on Sundays, but money can." This is a great quote! It simply means that money gets interest every day. It does not take a holiday or a sick day. Even when the banks are closed, the bank is paying a daily interest on your money. Did you ever try and call your bank and say, "Hey tomorrow is Christmas and everything is closed, can you credit me the interest on my mortgage for that day?" I bet you never even thought about that, did you? (Don't bother trying, however, I would imagine that they will not honor the request.)

So what does this mean?

Let's examine this idea for a minute. Imagine you go to a fortune teller, and every prediction this fortune teller has ever told has come true, with years and years and years of proof. She tells you that your newborn baby is guaranteed to win the 1 million dollar lottery before or on the day he or she reaches the age of 65 (I bet you forgot that this book has something to do with winning the lottery). The fortune teller cannot tell you the exact day, but she says you must play the lottery for the child every day, for if you miss even one day you are sure to have those numbers come up on that day, the one you do not play. Remember this fortune teller is never wrong; would you play the lottery every day, even it meant you might have to play every single day for the next 65 years for the child?

If you would, then think about this: if you were to start an investment account for your child the year he or she were born, and put in a dollar a day, or $365 a year, every year for 65 years with a investment interest rate of about 8.5%, on your child's 65th birthday he or she would have over 1 million dollars in that account. To really understand this phenomenon, you should realize that you only deposited $23,725 in this account. The interest made by this hard working, 7-day-a-week worker named "money" was over $995,000.

How many hours do you need to work to make that? In the example of the $17/ hour worker, it would take 58,416 hours or 25 years at that rate to make that money. Of course you have living expenses, so you would need that much more to be able to actually accumulate that million plus dollars in 25 years.

Now take this rule and remember this synopsis of the rule. You don't work for *money*; you work for *things* over time. Money, however, works for you and it makes *you* money over time.

RULE 3
"Stretch a dollar."

How far can you make the spending power of your dollar work for you? I recently read the Warren Buffett biography, *Snowball*, and was amazed that far into Mr. Buffet's accumulation of money, his wife Suzy was cutting coupons and saving pennies for everyday items. Now understand that Warren Buffett was at times the richest man in America, and his wife was using coupons!

When you purchase something, it is good to shop around and get the best price. I have found through the years that shopping for something secondhand from websites like eBay has saved me thousands.

Most of the time you can find the exact item that you are looking for in perfect condition, or even brand new, for huge discounts. Sometimes it even has the manufacturer's warranty along with it. Imagine if you could work only 100 hours for that HDTV instead of 147 hours. That makes it very clear.

The newness wears off pretty quickly anyway, and it becomes a used item to you as soon as you turn it on for the first time. In the case of a car, you could save thousands by buying a used car instead of a showroom new car. The only difference will be that you will get the car with that first ding already in it. On average, a 2-year-old car costs about 40% less than the original sticker price. Now that is a bargain!

I recently watched a brilliant television commercial about a person shopping for an item in a store. He was ready to buy the item but to be sure he wasn't paying too much he used his cell phone with Internet access to look up the competitors' prices. So when you are shopping, use the resources that you have, such as discount coupons, discount clubs like Sam's club or Costco, or any money-saving resource to make your cost lower. Don't be too proud to stretch or save a dollar.

Find the bargains and remember: it is your money, so use it wisely.

This brings me to the next rule....

RULE 4
"A penny saved is a penny earned."

For most Americans, we operate our households without any budget whatsoever. We simply "wing it"! This means that we have no idea how much we spend on any part of our life. A budget should be set up, followed, and adjusted for all who want a better financial life. We will be getting into budgets in a future chapter, but let's assume you have one so that we can go on with this rule.

If your grocery budget was a fixed amount of, let's say, $250 a month and you truly kept to that budget, this would mean that every month, month after month, you would spend exactly $250 on your groceries. This is difficult to imagine for most of you, but within reason it can be done. Now let's say you have a coupon for $2.00 off an item, another for $.50 off, and others that add up to a so-called savings of about $9.75 total. Your budget allows for $250, but you only spent $240.25; that means you have an extra $9.75. The question is what to do with this extra.

Most people would simply let it get *absorbed* into their daily mindless spending. It is my suggestion that you immediately transfer that $9.75 into your savings account. If you do this it will appear, at first, to be silly, but if you add up all of the places you can be saving and adding to this account, it will become a substantial amount over time.

How about that loose change in your pocket that ends up in the wash or even thrown out? You should be placing this into your change jar and whenever it is at a certain level you should count it and deposit it into your savings account. Each year, I count my "coffee can money" and it is well into the $300 range. Remember the example of $365/ year saved at 8.4% interest? It gave you over $1,000,000 in 65 years. If you don't have 65 years, then this is the reason to add your excess savings into this account to make it work for you as well. You will quickly find that this savings truly adds up.

You need to remember that it is not saved until it is *saved*. This means that you must put that savings away in a safe place. You must have an investment account or at least a simple savings account at a local bank to put this savings into. So if you do not have a specific account where you put aside extra money—not spending money, but particular savings money—then open that account today.

My suggestion is an online trading account or savings account, an account that does not have a checkbook or ATM card. The account can be added to online with a few keystrokes. This makes it very convenient as well as easy to remember to add to the account each time you save money, and because there is no checkbook or ATM card it is difficult to take the money out. You should never take from this account unless you have a sound place to make your money work for you; then and only then should you use this money.

Always remember that for every 100 pennies there is a dollar that can go to work for you, never asking for a day off or calling in sick. If you kick it to the side it will go work for someone else who picks it up. Make sure you treat it with the respect it deserves!

RULE 5
"Put your money where your mouth is."

I cannot tell you of all the investment advice I get from everyone I meet. I find it so amazing that there are so many people who claim to be experts when it comes to investing money. How many of your friends tell you of a great place to put your money? Do they have a great stock tip or say, "Now is the time to invest!"? Now think about this, how many times do you say this to your friends?

Everyone is an expert until they have to put their own money on the table for this PFA advice. PFA is simply "plucked from air" advice.

Even more important to remember is that if it is such great advice then you should keep it to yourself, not give away your secret for someone else to use before you have the opportunity to.

Imagine you discovered the recipe for a great pasta sauce and there was a fair in town that was having a contest for the best sauce. The first prize was $10,000 and you knew your sauce was the best. Of course you entered the contest, but you forgot that you bragged about your sauce and the ingredients so often that five of your neighbors entered the contest with their version of your sauce recipe. When the judges taste all of the sauces, they pick as the winner a basic and bland sauce because all of the other sauces tasted the same. You go home without the grand prize.

It is the same with investment ideas. If you have your eye on that abandoned property around the corner, and you are thinking about buying it and fixing it, then just do it. Don't brag to everyone you meet about buying it instead of actually buying it. When you do this, just when you get the nerve to buy it, you will find that one of the people you told about it is now the owner.

Also, if you are truly doing well in an investment, don't brag about it. Even the Bible makes a reference to this in James 4:16: "But you boast about your proud intentions. All such boasting is evil." And it truly is. If you have a great idea then do it; don't brag about it.

If you want to win big at the casino tables, look at the person making the most noise, then wait a few minutes and bet against them. Time after time the big winner, the one making all of the noise, is soon the big loser. Look around and you will find the quiet ones often have a pile of money in front of them. If you have ever been at a casino you understand what I am referring to. By the way, that last statement should not be taken as advice, just an illustration.

Even recently, my hero Warren Buffett was speaking about the economy. Buffett is usually the silent type. He usually does his thing and makes his stock picks or investments his business with little discussion to the public. When Buffett started buying crazy over-priced stocks and bragging about it, the stocks tanked! The oracle of Omaha had broken this rule and sure enough he lost billions. Now don't feel sorry for Buffett because he still is the richest man in the world, but just understand that when you brag you are soon going to cry.

RULE 6
"Money doesn't grow on trees."

Every fall you see so many people with their leaf blowers and rakes, blowing or pushing aside and then collecting and bagging the leaves that fall from trees. I have often looked, but as hard as I look, I never see any dollars falling from trees.

Now I am sure you are finding this rule obvious and as the other rules start to sink in this rule is, well, kind of predictable, isn't it? Well, read on....

In the heyday of the 2000's there was actually a lending institute that called itself "Lending Tree." I would bet most of you just went "aha," because you realize the comparison of how people actually borrowed money like it was growing on trees!

The company was actually teasing you by inferring that money did grow on trees. I even believe that the symbol for the company was a "money tree." You simply went to the "tree," the local or online bank, and peeled off the money on the branches of the tree. That tree is and was never real. If money comes from anywhere that it is not earned, then it is not yours and has little value. Money is always earned, no exceptions! It does not grow on trees, or in the garden, or anywhere else; it is only earned by your time, or your money's time, spent earning it.

RULE 7
"There's gold in them thar hills."

America is and will always be the land of opportunity. This is the land where people can become overnight millionaires. If you have watched shows like "American Idol," "Who Wants to be a Millionaire," or "Deal or No Deal," you can understand just some of the opportunities that are available in "them thar hills."

Okay, I understand that not all of us are ready to compete in television shows like these. However, there are so many opportunities to make money or to get other riches. America, and the rest of the world, is filled with ideas both conceived and not yet conceived that can make you rich or happy. The difference between the people who bring these ideas to the world and those who don't is simply a desire to do it.

If you truly want something or want to make it happen, then just do it! I have devoted other chapters to this very subject and you will soon learn about how to put your desires to work for you. Desires, like money, also work on holidays and weekends and can grow into your richest monetary dreams.

So these are the clichés / rules that you should consider at all times. This very foundation will start you on the path to having more riches and less worries in a short period of time.

Here is a summary of these positive clichés:

"Another day, another dollar."

Go out and earn everyday. Don't be too proud to earn less; just earn.

"Time is money."

You don't work for money; *you work for* things *over time. Money, however, works for you and it makes* you *money over time.*

"Stretch a dollar."

Use coupons and truly shop for a bargain. It is your money; spend it wisely.

"A penny saved is a penny earned."

Save your pennies! Turn them into dollars and let them work for you.

"Put your money where your mouth is."

Go out and do it, don't just talk about it.

"Money doesn't grow on trees."

Money is earned by working for it and putting it to work for you. You can't rake it in like leaves fallen from a tree.

"There's gold in them thar hills".

Always remember that this is the land of opportunity and yours awaits you if you are open to it.

Now for my next set of lottery numbers.

Remember to read these out loud, please!

5 21 24 40 44 Powerball 11

Chapter 3

"A Fool and His Money are Soon Parted"

As with any relationship, your relationship with money needs to grow and be nurtured. If you treat money poorly or cheat on money, or simply ignore money, it will go away. Most people go through life living paycheck to paycheck, never really thinking about money or the concept of money. Like in any selfish relationship, all people think about is me me me. "What can I buy today for instant gratification?" "How can my money make me happy today?" "Whom can I impress with my money?"

Remember the Grimm fairy tale of the golden goose? In this fairy tale, a farmer who was struggling financially found that his goose laid a golden egg. He couldn't believe his eyes! The egg was worth a fortune. He then found that the next day the goose laid another golden egg!

Now each day the farmer would find another egg laid by the goose and the farmer was getting richer and richer. Now the farmer, who just months ago was just about broke, was living in riches. New fancy clothes, new fancy house, new fancy car (there were no cars when this story was written, so this is my interpretation of the story), and he also going out and having a great time. Never saving or thinking about saving because he knew that the goose would lay another egg tomorrow.

Now the story goes on that the farmer was getting impatient and wanted the goose to lay more eggs, but to the farmer's chagrin, the goose would only lay one egg each day. He, who was poor only a few months ago, now had golden eggs and a better, richer lifestyle, but unfortunately, it wasn't enough for him. He was starting to get greedy. He wanted more and more! The house wasn't big enough and the car already had a dent in it. He wanted a bigger house and a nicer car! Nothing was good enough and the next bigger or better thing was waiting for him. His lack of patience and greed was overwhelming him. So now what?

Well if you have read the fable, then you know that the farmer decided to cut open the goose to fetch all of the eggs. To his surprise there were no eggs inside and of course the goose was now dead, leaving the farmer with nothing more than a dead goose and no more golden eggs.

Recently, Oprah Winfrey had a special segment on her show, discussing the new "tent cities" in California. The residents of tent cities are typically people who have lost their homes due to foreclosure and have lost their jobs with little hope of finding one quickly. By the name you can surmise that these people are literally living in tents. There are so many tents concentrated in one area that they are referred to as a "tent city." The tent city is a place to live for now. This is a very sad state for these people and their families. Tent cities were also a part of the Great Depression and food lines soon followed. These times have returned and hopefully they will be a past memory to those reading this book.

In the Oprah Winfrey show, the people living in this situation all said the same thing when asked, "What would you have done differently?" They all said, "I would have saved or put away some money."

Impatience, pride, and greed are all the farmer's flaws in the goose story. Think about this new ending to the story: what if the famer didn't kill the goose? Would the goose live forever? How many golden eggs would you have saved if you thought that some day that goose would die? How many years should a goose live? And what if the goose simply stopped laying the golden eggs? Would you be prepared? Well, this has happened for many Americans. The goose is gone or dead or stopped laying eggs. So now what?

The only hope that they (we) have is that, as long you have your health and desires, there is another goose waiting in the barn for you. The question is, how will you treat this goose? Will you cut it open to take all you can? Or will you treat it well and feed it the finest goose feed? Will you remember that, no matter how well you treat the goose, one day it too will die of old age?

In the last chapter, I discussed the rules of money one should follow, as expressed in clichés; the following clichés are cautionary clichés. These are clichés you should think about when the next goose arrives (and I assure you that it will). I also caution you to make sure that you recognize it when it does. The "golden goose" may come in the form of something obvious like a new job or an inheritance or a lottery winning. It may also be something subtle like an employee benefit or a government grant or maybe just an idea. Either way, make sure that you cherish it and remember that the goose, like you and your health and young age, will not last forever. So read them carefully and be mindful of them at all times.

CAUTIONARY RULE 1
"Money is burning a hole in my pocket."

I remember a birthday when I was about 9 or 10 years old and for the first time that I can recall, I had money for my birthday. You know, real money, the kind of money that was so much money that everyone would wish they were me, the real moo-la, the big bucks, you know... twenty dollars! At least to a 10–year-old in 1973 that was a lot of money. I couldn't wait to go spend it. I wanted to buy games and candy and the latest toy. I think it was the "Evil Knievel Stunt Cycle" or something like that. I was so excited that I couldn't contain myself and tried everything to get my mother to take me to the toy store. I remember my mother saying, "Is the money burning a hole in your pocket?"

I was 10, so I didn't care too much about this. Heck, the golden goose, my mother, was going to feed me and shelter me long after the money was spent and those toys I bought were in the garbage. That 20 bucks was going to be spent quickly on all the frivolous things that a 10-year-old buys and never a second thought would be given to it until, of course, I sat down and wrote this book.

Think about the countless times you have had extra money. Maybe this money was an inheritance or a bonus at work, a tax refund or a birthday gift. Or maybe you found a 10 dollar bill in the street. What did you do with it? Was it "burning a hole in your pocket"?

A little extra cash in your pocket often leads to frivolous spending. Now this spending can be anything. I am guilty of this and often find myself walking out of a convenience store with a candy bar or a sandwich or a hot dog when all I really wanted was a coffee. Now I have spent about $4 for a $1 cup of coffee, all because the money was "burning a hole in my pocket."

Now think about your credit cards and how they are in your wallet wherever you go. I remember once going to a casino and my friend said, "Before we leave, I want to take my credit cards out of my wallet." When I asked why, his answer was obvious and simple. He explained that, if and when he ran out of money by gambling it away, he would look to take cash advances against his credit cards to continue playing. Now you can imagine that if he had 3 or 4 credit cards with limits of $10,000, and he brought them with him, he could get himself into a lot of trouble.

Now think about this: if you bring credit cards with you wherever you go, then that available credit is also "burning a hole in your pocket." Your ability to become an impulse buyer is unchecked.   Have you ever walked into a store, just to waste some time or to window shop, and found that a one-of-a-kind bargain was presented to you on something you'd only thought about buying? You know what happens next....

There it is, a TV that is big and bold. This is the TV you thought about or saw at a friend's house or read about in a trade magazine.   You had no intention of buying this today or even had no plans to buy it ever, but there it is and 20% off, yours for a simple swipe of your credit card. So what do you do? You buy it, of course! No thought to the rule that "**time is money,**" no thought to how much interest it will cost, no thought to how the payments will be made. You didn't even call your spouse; after all, she will love it because it is a great TV! You load it into your car and proudly set it up once you get home.

Then what happens? Your spouse screams, and when your credit card statement comes your payment is high and the balance is high. Because of all this, the TV just doesn't look as good as it did in the store. As a matter of fact, the whole instant gratification thing isn't so gratifying anymore and you wish you had never bought that constant reminder of why you are broke.

The solution is to think about the gambler who leaves his credit card home.   Take with you only the amount of money you need for the day, and take the credit cards out of your wallet. I know what you are thinking: what about an emergency? What if my car breaks down and I need to get a tow or a fix a tire? I assure you that you can work this problem out. You may have a family member at home or friend who can bring you the card or you may be able to go home and get it after the repairs are made. If you truly are afraid, then only leave one credit card in your wallet. This credit card should have a low limit such as $500 or $1000—and only use this for an emergency, not for impulse buying!

As far as money goes, and I mean actual cash, you should have the same thought and discipline. Only carry what you need for the day with you. If you need money for lunch, then bring only the amount you need for lunch. If you need gas for your car, then bring the cash for the gas. Do not use your emergency credit card—or any credit card—for gas. I know it is easier to just swipe the card through the reader but you will find that you will be a better saver by using cash for gas. You will save in two ways. The first is very noticeable, in that most gas stations will give a discount for cash. The second is the interest you will save by not putting it on your charge card balance.

As another added bonus, you will be more aware of the money you are spending on gas. You may actually drive less or more efficiently because you are aware that you are spending money, not just swiping a plastic card.

Think twice about money. If it is truly "burning a hole in your pocket," then take it out of your pocket, NOW! Deposit it into your savings account. Think about someone in the tent cities or maybe your own situation: would this money that once burned a hole in their or your pocket be useful now? Think about your retirement: how would the Evil Kinevel Stunt Cycle help me or you to buy food when the golden egg of earning has long since gone? Let the money fire a retirement fund or an emergency fund, not burn a hole in your pocket.

CAUTIONARY RULE 2,
"Penny wise and pound foolish."

When purchasing an item or picking a service, we sometimes forget that the price is not always the best indicator to determine if we are getting a bargain.

I mentioned eBay as a great place to pick up great deals. However, with eBay and other places that are oozing with discounts, the product may not be what it appears. I am currently writing this book using a computer monitor that has an annoying flicker. You see, one day I was in an office supply super store and there it was, a new 22-inch monitor. Okay it wasn't exactly new, it was a demo, but heck, it was 20% off and with "money burning a hole in my pocket" I bought it. Well about 6 months later it started to flicker. Not badly enough for me to throw it away, but badly enough for me to notice it and think about the $40 I could have put toward the brand new one in the box and not have to be annoyed with this flicker (or maybe I should have left my credit card home that day, but that is another story).

I have an uncle who is always thinking about saving a buck. He also buys bargains, only *his* bargains are food bargains. He will buy the food that is either expired or about to expire because it is often 30% to 50% less expensive. The problem with this is that he is often throwing away food that is rotting in his refrigerator. Now is that really a bargain?

If you think about the actual syntax of the cliché, you may even think that bulk food buying is also a good idea. Many of the big chain food stores or discount warehouses offer you pounds of food for a discount price. At any one time these stores are packed with people buying 20 pound bags of cereal or 4 gallons of milk in a carry case or 30 eggs all because the price per unit is smaller. Is this truly a good idea?

In theory the concept is great, as long as you or your family can use these products before they expire or go stale. But beware: if you find yourself throwing away lots of food, then you are seriously being pound foolish and not penny wise.

Reading this, you may think that bargain shopping isn't such a great idea. Sometimes it is and sometimes it isn't. I recently came across a great concept: being mindful. Simply put, to be mindful is to think about your situation and how your next purchase will affect that situation. If you are at the bulk store and want to buy that 3 pound bag of cereal, be mindful of how long it will take to eat it. Do you eat it often? Do you like it enough to own all of that? Where are you going to keep it? Be mindful of these questions and others when you buy in bulk.

So what about services? Sometimes it is better to hire the right person for the job. Did you ever try to hire a handyman to fix a real problem with your home? Maybe it was a plumbing problem or a roof leak. You hire this guy who pulls up in a beat-up truck with lots of beat-up tools and he climbs your roof to try and fix the leak. Now this leak has been ruining your bedroom ceiling for the last 3 weeks and has caused you to send your favorite comforter to the cleaners to get the water stains out of it.

The handyman climbs up and is on the roof for about an hour. He is banging and clanging and is doing all kinds of stuff up there. He comes down and says, "All fixed." He hands you a bill that was probably about $75 less than a local roofer and is on his way, and you are relieved.

So you pick up the comforter from the dry cleaner, you patch and paint the ceiling and your problems are over. At least, that is what you think at the time.

A few days later it rains, and I mean it really rains. You know, sheeting rain and thunder. Only it's not the thunder that wakes you up, it is the puddle in your bed from the roof leak that wasn't fixed properly at all. Now your $75 savings is well lost in your need to hire the right person for the job.

Keep in mind, though, that while this is such a great rule to consider when purchasing anything, be very cautious with this "wolf in sheep's clothing" cliché. It is often used as an excuse to "buy up" instead of save. How many times have you decided to buy the more expensive item because you felt it was better? That stove is better because it has a stainless steel cooking rack or that car is better because it has rear seat warmers or that computer has a media center. You spend the extra few dollars not to be pound foolish because those "might as wells" or add-ons are so great. Of course you hardly cook, so the stainless steel has little or no value. You almost never carry rear seat passengers so the heated rear seat goes unused and of course you only use your computer for word processing or internet surfing and really don't need the media player.

But heck, these things are cheap add-ons so you buy them with the excuse of not being pound foolish.

A buzzer should go off in your head when you are making these decisions. Be aware of the hours of work you save by being penny wise, but make sure you are truly penny wise and not pound foolish.

CAUTIONARY RULE 3
"Blood money."

This is the worst kind of money of all. This cautionary rule applies to two types of money sourcing. The first comes from the meaning of the cliché itself. Money that was received from criminal activity is often referred to as blood money. The reference came from the fact that someone was murdered to acquire it, therefore blood was spilled, hence the phrase "blood money." Money acquired by any means that is not honest should be considered "blood money." If you cheat or steal to acquire money you will surely never be able to handle the guilt. It will haunt you forever and I assure you that you will get caught or the guilt will cause you to not truly enjoy the gifts that the money can bring without an unfortunate ending. Is it true that some people can be millionaires or even billionaires with "blood money"? I am afraid it is, but for how long and at what price?

Bernard Madoff has become one of the most successful thieves in modern history. He was in charge of billions of dollars deposited by investors in his hedge fund. It turns out that Madoff was stealing this money and not investing it at all. His method of stealing was that of an old trickster named Charles Ponzi. Madoff, like Ponzi, was forging statements to his investors. These "snake oil" salesmen simply sold the dream of ridiculously high rates of returns. In Madoff's case many of the people he defrauded were friends. He stole from his friends about 50 billion dollars total. You can surely understand the amount of pain this man has caused the investors. Some, who were millionaires, are now completely broke.

There is a story of a woman who kept all of her money with Madoff. She was elderly, in her late 60's, and thought that she was financially set to live the rest of her life in comfort. Madoff had all of her seven million dollars and now she has nothing. This woman now cleans houses just so she can buy food. I am sure that you can understand why she cried for days after her first day of work.

It is clear to understand how the victims suffer from the acquisition of blood money, but what about the thief? There are countless stories of people who feel the desperation of money troubles and decide to steal to relieve the pain. It is a fact that in these trying times of the 2009 recession/depression, crime rates have in fact increased. The problem with these stories is that they end in disaster for the thief. Jail is not the place to enjoy your life, and that is where most of these people end up. Remember that even if you think you are stealing for the good of your family, your family will live a worse life if you are in jail. The disgrace alone could harm a child for many years into their adult life.

If we go back to the example of Bernard Madoff, his family will pay the price for years after. Who would want to associate with the children of this thief? His wife is having her house confiscated and all of her money is being scrutinized. Can you imagine the life of Bernard Madoff in jail? This criminal is accustomed to high-society living and the people whom he associated with are clearly different than the people whom he now shares a jail cell with. Madoff will die in jail, unless he outlives his 150-year sentence. Going into the sentence at 70 years old makes that highly unlikely. I am sure that he wakes up everyday, like some of his victims, wishing he didn't wake up at all.

CAUTIONARY RULE 3A (*THE OTHER TYPE OF BLOOD MONEY*)
Never do business with family or friends.

Borrowing money from relatives or lending money to relatives is another type of "blood money" to avoid. The complications of lending money to relatives have led to all kinds of troubles.

Imagine this scenario. Your sister comes to you and says her family is in trouble, they need $1000 to fix their oil heater in the dead of winter. You have the money, and after all you love this person, so you give her the money. The source of this money may have even been a true sacrifice for you, but after all this is someone you love and care for and everyone wants to be there when someone we love truly needs us. Maybe you were saving that money in your untouchable account (we will get into this later) or you had that money put away for a special purpose, like a new computer. Or maybe you borrowed the money from your credit card or home equity loan to help your sister in this predicament. After all, she has two small kids and they are your nieces. You wouldn't want them to freeze, would you? So you turn over the money. She fixes her heat and you feel great.

Now about 4 weeks goes by and you have this $1000 credit card bill at something like 18% interest and you ask her to pay it. Of course she gives you the story about how the rent is due and kids are sick and so on. So you pay the bill on your own and wait for her to pay you back. It doesn't take long for you to realize that you are not going to be paid back any time soon and your bitterness toward your sister starts. Now 3 or 4 months have gone by and you have paid 3 or 4 payments on this "thousand dollars" credit card balance and you are getting downright angry. Now the spring is here and the memory of the heater being broken is long gone from your sister's memory. Your bill at 18% is of course continuing to nag you.

Finally one day your sister calls you up. She is so excited, she can't wait to come over and tell you the great news! You are so happy because what else can the good news be; she must have your money. So now you can't wait until she gets here and you are so happy that this is finally over. You even think about telling her how upset you were just so you can apologize and feel better.

Then it happens. She comes to the door with a big smile on her face and points out her new car parked in front of the driveway! Now you start to get a little upset because you were disappointed that this isn't about the money she owes and here comes the fireworks. She tells you how excited she is because she only had to put down $1000 and make the rest in payments over the next 6 or 7 years of $375 a month.

You have just reached your boiling point and you flip out! How dare she? For the last 4 months she could have given you that $375 to pay back the money she owed, and what about the thousand dollars she put down on the car? That was the amount she owed you, at least the principal anyway. You look over at your old car and after a huge argument, you close the door on your sister for the last time and probably never speak to her again.

Just to rub it in more, think about this. What if you were the sister? Your thoughts would be that my sister is a nasty, terrible person for not speaking to me. How dare she hate me over money? After all, I needed that car because my car was about to die. I needed that car almost as badly as I needed my heater in the dead of winter. Forget her; I will never pay her now!

If you don't believe this happens, just watch Judge Judy and you will find these cases at least once a month on her show. Now if you ever feel that you must lend money to a friend or relative, make sure that you have devised a definite plan to have the money returned, and discuss and put in writing the rules in which it was lent or borrowed. Take collateral if you must, but make sure everyone knows the rules upfront.

The rules and expectations are the most important things to put in writing. Is it okay for your sister to buy something big, like a car, if she owes you money? What are the payment terms and the penalties for late payments, and how will you enforce payment? These are all of the thoughts you should consider when you lend money to a friend or relative.

Even our government has made this mistake recently when a big insurance company was lent $160 billion dollars to keep the company from going bankrupt. This money was the AIG bailout. The government pretty much lent the money without any rules, and then the big problems started to come. Remember the bonuses paid to key employees and the extravagant trips for other employees? The American people became a mob to protest these bonuses. The taxpayers paid for those bailouts; how dare the company give the money to the employees and not pay back the government.

Now the government starts to make rules after the money is already given or lent, and now everyone is suffering. The people who expected those bonuses and frankly counted on them are in financial trouble, the government officials are having their resignations asked for, and any company who may need a bailout in the future has little chance of getting one. Even legislation to avoid paying bonuses to employees in bailed-out companies is in the works. What a mess this "blood money" cost, all because the expectations and rules were not discussed upfront.

So what does this mean? It is simple: have respect and honesty in all money dealings. Be honest in your intentions and if you truly must borrow money from a relative, make sure you both understand that it is a business transaction with rules set forth *before* the transaction, not after. This will protect both parties from the sorrow that often is caused by good intentions. But, most importantly, avoid borrowing or lending money to relatives or friends.

…That brings me to the next rule…

CAUTIONARY RULE 4
"Money is the root of all evil."

Most people do not understand that this true cliché is actually a Bible phrase and it goes like this: *"for the love of money is the root of all evil"* 1 Timothy 6:10.

This is a very important distinction from the cliché that has been derived from it. Money is definitely not evil or the root of all evil; instead it is the *love* of money that is the root of all evil. What is important about this cliché or Bible quote is not the object (money) itself; it is the jealousy, greed and fear associated with the love of or desire for money.

As I have said before, it is my goal to accumulate and distribute as much money as I can. I will not make the love of money or the material things it can buy more important than life itself. Nor will I allow myself to be jealous or envious of the things that others have.

A portion of lyrics from the song called "For the Love of Money" by the O'Jays is as follows:

> *For the love of money*
> *People will steal from their mother*
> *For the love of money*
> *People will rob their own brother*

These lyrics are an expression of the outcome of jealousy, greed, and fear. The saddest part of this is that money does not make people who love money, or love the accumulation of money, happy. Their desire to own it, or their covetousness of it, actually makes them miserable. Think about the reality of this thought: *You cannot have all of the money in the world—and if you did, then it would be worthless anyway.* This means that people who are obsessed with money can never be satisfied, simply because there is always more money to be had.

The greatest story to describe this was written by Charles Dickens in the novel *A Christmas Carol*. Remember Ebenezer Scrooge? Was he happy? His entre life was devoted to the collection of money. He had, as we were led to believe, more money than anyone at the time—and he was truly miserable. In the case of Scrooge, he had to show compassion and love before he could be happy. What Scrooge discovers is that companionship and love cost nothing, but they are priceless.

Jealousy and greed (love of money) are what took America into the problems of the Great Depression of the 1930's and the great recession/depression of 2009. It is the love of money or the love of the things that money could buy that caused so many people to over-buy and leverage their houses and credit cards. If my neighbor can buy that Mercedes, well then I should have one also. If my neighbor has a pool, then I should have one also. If my neighbor moved to a bigger house, well then I will also.

Jealousy and greed are easy to understand by the above examples, but what about the fear of not having money? This fear is one that often leads to losing money. It causes the trickster to make others part with their money. This leads to some crazy ideas on how to accumulate wealth quickly. Have you ever received an e-mail from your long-lost relative in someplace like Malaysia or Africa, and he asked for $10,000 so he could get $10,000,000 that is waiting for him in some account? And for your kindness in lending him the $10,000, he would give you $1,000,000?

Did you know that people actually send the money? This is the product of fear of poverty. They believe the "get-rich-quick schemes" of the wicked. Some may have found the book or system that will make them a fortune in the stock market or a book on gambling that is guaranteed to make them a fortune. They then lose it all and all of this happens because of their love of money.

You always need to remember that any obsession will cause great harm to you mentally as well as financially. Remember not to love money but instead to treat money like any relationship: with caring and mindfulness.

These are the cautionary rules of money. I am sure that you had found that you experienced some of these problems with money in your past. I hope that you have an understanding of these rules and will be cautious in your new relationship with money.

Here is a summary of these cautionary clichés;

"Money is burning a hole in my pocket."

Keep money from "burning a hole in your pocket" by leaving it home, or even better, in an account where it can work for you.

"Penny wise and pound foolish."

Don't skimp where it is important, but don't use this rule as an excuse to buy more than you need.

"Blood money."

Stealing or getting money illegally will never allow you to have the joy that money earned honestly will allow. There are so many ways to make money legally; don't waste your energy on the illegal ways.

Be cautious when doing business with family or friends (the other blood money).

Avoid lending to friends and family, but if you must, make sure all terms and expectations are fully understood and in writing.

"Money is the root of all evil."

Money is not evil; it is the love of money that can make someone evil. Don't be jealous of others and what others have; instead be grateful for what you have. Remember that there is always someone who has more than you, but more importantly remember that there is always someone who has less, a lot less, than you do.

Now for my next set of lottery numbers.

Remember to read these out loud, please!
14 25 29 43 48 Powerball 11

Chapter 4

The Balanced Budget

Have you ever met that person who truly has no money problems? I don't mean that they didn't wish they had more. This is the person who never has to borrow money to pay bills or to buy a car or even to buy house. Have you ever met what some refer to as *The Millionaire Next Door*[1]?

These are the people who truly have no substantial money problems whatsoever. They live among us like aliens or a different species that the rest of us can't understand. They have credit scores of 800 and higher, they have little or even no mortgages, absolutely do not have a car loan, and of course never have credit card bills. They are the "others."

The hardest thing to understand about the "others" is that they usually have modest incomes. The rest of us have nothing saved, high mortgages and usually make more than twice what the "others" make. They are usually school teachers or government workers or hold other medium- to low-paying jobs while some of us are making well into the 6 figures and have nothing! How do the "others" do it?

We are told time and time again that these people "*live well below their means.*" Live below their means? How can they do that? How can they live next door to you in the same style home while making less money than you, while you can barely pay your bills at your higher salary? How can it be? What is it that makes them the "others"?

The answer is **discipline**.

Discipline is one of those elusive words that make us cringe. To many of us the word *discipline* is associated with pain. Remember when your parents were "disciplining" you? It often meant some type of punishment.

Wikipedia defines "discipline" as follows:

To discipline thus means to instruct a person or animal to follow a particular code of conduct, or to adhere to a certain order. Discipline refers to methods of modeling character and of teaching self-control and acceptable behavior.

That is a much softer version of the definition of discipline than we are used to. If we examine the words "teaching self-control" and say that it is time "we" learned some self-control, we can, in time, become one of the "others." If we assume that the "others" have discipline, then it is time to outline disciplines for becoming free of the burdens of being broke.

The very first discipline to learn is "pay yourself first." This is another one of those elusive statements that needs to be fully understood. I first heard this statement while I was in business for myself. I went to a seminar that talked about running a business more effectively. The speaker said that, when you get any receivables (payments from clients), you should pay yourself first. This makes sense because, after all, we are in business to make some money to have or to spend for ourselves, not just to pay our bills for our business.

As time went on, I heard this phrase again. This time it was the 401K representative talking about how if you sign up for a 401k, you will pay yourself first automatically. Now I was truly confused. I thought that if I was no longer in business for myself, then every paycheck was "paying me first."

So, what does it really mean to "pay yourself first"? How do we truly become one of the "others" by paying ourselves first?

In a previous chapter, I briefly mentioned an untouchable account. This is an account that you simply, well, do not touch. Money goes into this account and does not come out. It is okay to think of this account as a retirement account or an emergency fund, but money should never come out of this account during the time you are accumulating or earning money. This is where you pay yourself first.

The amount of money that goes into this account should be no less than 10% of your gross pay from any source. That means if you make $45,000 a year, $4,500 should be put into this account for that year. Do not make the mistake of trying to put that money in the account at the end of the year; it simply won't happen. The 10% should be put in from each and every paycheck immediately upon receiving it. My preference is to have my paycheck directly deposited into my checking account and then the 10% withdrawn automatically into the untouchable account. An online brokerage account or online bank account is perfect for this. Remember, do not get a debit card or a checkbook for this account. The debit card and checkbook will make it too easy to withdraw the funds and the money will be *burning a hole in your pocket.*

Putting away 10% requires discipline and in a short time will give you the true rewards of the "others." I can already read your mind. The first thing you are thinking is: "Yeah right" how do I put away 10% when I can't even pay my bills now?" Or you may be thinking: "I already put 5% into my 401k, and my company matches it, so isn't that good enough?" My answer? Put the 10% away from every income source, every time. "Pay yourself first!" If you do have a 401k or similar plan, it is okay to use the portion that you are contributing as part of the 10%. For example, if you are putting in 5% into your 401K, then you now must put away another 5% in an untouchable account. It is certainly a good idea to put away more if you can, but at least 10% should always be put away.

Remember that there are also other sources of income or money that come into your life. Take all of them, the birthday money sent by your grandmother, the $20 bill you found on the street, the part-time handyman work that paid you cash: all of it and always with no exceptions goes into this account. My personal rule is that with all secondary income sources I receive, I put 50% in my untouchable account. That means if I receive a birthday gift of $25 I put $12.50 in the account and spend the rest. My tax refund, 50% goes in the untouchable account. If I win $100 in the lottery, $50 goes into the untouchable account and the rest gets spent. I am currently on salary and commission at my current employment. Each commission check gets cut in half. 50% goes into the untouchable account and 50% gets spent.

You must truly understand that this 10% is the most important part of the discipline. It comes first. It comes before you pay anyone or any bill. It comes before your housing payment or your car payment or even your electric bill. Make sure you fully understand this principle and soon you will become one of the "others."

The next discipline is to pay off your debts. 20% of your salary goes toward your debts. No more than 20%. Read that again: no more than 20% goes toward your debts. That means if you are earning $45,000 a year, you are paying $9,000 toward paying off your debts. This includes all debts except for the primary mortgage on your home. The primary mortgage will be paid for out of the 70% that is left.

Some questions are sure to arise from this concept. The first and most likely is, "What if my minimum payments on my debts are more than 20% of my pay?" This is where you truly need to change your thinking. We are convinced that something terrible will happen to us if we do not make the exact payment that the bank or credit card company has asked of us. This is simply not true. No more than 20% goes to pay off your debts. If you need to call your debtors and renegotiate, then do it. If they are not receptive then try to accommodate them by negotiating with other debtors. If you can't negotiate with any of them, have the discipline to pay them less anyway. I assure you that in the end you will be happier and the debtor will be paid off eventually, making them satisfied as well.

It is best to pay the higher-interest debts more money so that you can pay them off first when possible. Most people do not understand the concept of paying interest. For example, if you have a credit card with an $8,600 balance and an average interest rate of 14% and pay the minimum payment, it will take you 20 years to pay it off and you will have paid over $17,000 in interest. If the interest was only 1% higher, 15%, then you would pay over $26,000 in interest. That one percentage point makes a big difference in your total interest payments.

Armed with this knowledge, it is clear that we want our loans to have the lowest possible interest rate at all times. The first step in paying off our debt is to get rid of the highest-interest debt as soon as possible.

This is a typical example of a $45,000-a-year earner with debts that are as follows:

Car loan balance	$14,600	interest of 9%	Payment $363.32
MasterCard balance	$8,600	interest of 14%	Payment $106.94
Personal loan	$15,000	interest of 12%	Payment $215.21
Department store card	$1,500	interest of 21%	Payment $27.46
		Monthly Total	$712.93

If you paid the minimum payments on these loans it would take up to 20 years to pay the final MasterCard payment. You would also pay a total of $34,173.54 in interest for debts of $39,700. This would bring you to a total of $73,873.54 in payments, more than double the amount you originally borrowed.

If you recall, the discipline is to pay 20% of your total income toward your debts each month. That means that if your salary is $45,000, then you should be paying $750 (45,000/12=$3750x2=$750), not $712.93, toward your debt each month until you are debt free. This means that you need to allocate an additional $37.07 toward the monthly payment of these bills.

You also should pay off your higher-interest debts first. That means you should pay off the department store credit card first. After each debt is paid in full you then take the difference and put it toward the next highest-interest debt, in this case the MasterCard, then the personal loan, and finally the car loan. Each time you pay off a debt you take the remainder of the $750 payment and put it toward the leftover debts.

Making the assumption that you start the program on June 2009, the payment schedule will look like what you see in the following payoff schedule. (You will find a payoff schedule spreadsheet for your personal use and other bonus materials at www.25milliondollarmasterminds.com. This website has several pieces of key information that accompanies this book.)

Payoff Schedule

Monthly Payment Amount	$750 month		
	Payment Amount	Balance	
Debt Name			
			Extra
Department store	$64.53	$1,461.72	$37.07
MasterCard	$106.94	$8,593.39	
personal loan	$215.22	$14,934.78	
car loan	$363.32	$14,346.18	
	Balance Total	$39,336.07	
Monthly Payment for June, 2009			
Department store	$64.53	$1,422.77	
MasterCard	$106.94	$8,586.71	
personal loan	$215.22	$14,868.91	
car loan	$363.32	$14,090.46	
	Total Balance	$38,968.85	
Monthly Payment for July, 2009			
Department store	$64.53	$1,383.14	
MasterCard	$106.94	$8,579.95	
personal loan	$215.22	$14,802.38	
car loan	$363.32	$13,832.82	
	Total Balance	$38,598.29	
Monthly Payment for August, 2009			
Department store	$64.53	$1,342.81	
MasterCard	$106.94	$8,573.11	
personal loan	$215.22	$14,735.18	
car loan	$363.32	$13,573.25	

| | Total Balance | $38,224.35 |

Monthly Payment for September, 2009

Department store	$64.53	$1,301.78
MasterCard	$106.94	$8,566.19
personal loan	$215.22	$14,667.31
car loan	$363.32	$13,311.73
	Total Balance	$37,847.01

Monthly Payment for
October, 2009

Department store	$64.53	$1,260.03
MasterCard	$106.94	$8,559.19
personal loan	$215.22	$14,598.76
car loan	$363.32	$13,048.25
	Total Balance	$37,466.23

Monthly Payment for
November, 2009

Department store	$64.53	$1,217.55
MasterCard	$106.94	$8,552.11
personal loan	$215.22	$14,529.53
car loan	$363.32	$12,782.79
	Total Balance	$37,081.98

Monthly Payment for
December, 2009

Department store	$64.53	$1,174.33
MasterCard	$106.94	$8,544.94
personal loan	$215.22	$14,459.61
car loan	$363.32	$12,515.34
	Total Balance	$36,694.22

Monthly Payment for
January, 2010

Department store	$64.53	$1,130.35
MasterCard	$106.94	$8,537.69
personal loan	$215.22	$14,388.99
car loan	$363.32	$12,245.89
	Total Balance	$36,302.92

Monthly Payment for February, 2010

Department store	$64.53	$1,085.60
MasterCard	$106.94	$8,530.36
personal loan	$215.22	$14,317.66
car loan	$363.32	$11,974.41
	Total Balance	$35,908.03

Monthly Payment for March, 2010

Department store	$64.53	$1,040.07
MasterCard	$106.94	$8,522.94
personal loan	$215.22	$14,245.62
car loan	$363.32	$11,700.90
	Total Balance	$35,509.53

Monthly Payment for April, 2010

Department store	$64.53	$993.74
MasterCard	$106.94	$8,515.43
personal loan	$215.22	$14,172.86
car loan	$363.32	$11,425.34
	Total Balance	$35,107.37

Monthly Payment for May, 2010

Department store	$64.53	$946.60
MasterCard	$106.94	$8,507.84
personal loan	$215.22	$14,099.37
car loan	$363.32	$11,147.71
	Total Balance	$34,701.52

Monthly Payment for June, 2010

Department store	$64.53	$898.64
MasterCard	$106.94	$8,500.16
personal loan	$215.22	$14,025.14
car loan	$363.32	$10,868.00
	Total Balance	$34,291.94

Monthly Payment for July, 2010

Department store	$64.53	$849.84
MasterCard	$106.94	$8,492.39

personal loan	$215.22	$13,950.17
car loan	$363.32	$10,586.19
	Total Balance	$33,878.59

Monthly Payment for August, 2010

Department store	$64.53	$800.18
MasterCard	$106.94	$8,484.53
personal loan	$215.22	$13,874.45
car loan	$363.32	$10,302.27
	Total Balance	$33,461.43

Monthly Payment for September, 2010

Department store	$64.53	$749.65
MasterCard	$106.94	$8,476.58
personal loan	$215.22	$13,797.97
car loan	$363.32	$10,016.22
	Total Balance	$33,040.42

Monthly Payment for October, 2010

Department store	$64.53	$698.24
MasterCard	$106.94	$8,468.53
personal loan	$215.22	$13,720.73
car loan	$363.32	$9,728.02
	Total Balance	$32,615.52

Monthly Payment for November, 2010

Department store	$64.53	$645.93
MasterCard	$106.94	$8,460.39
personal loan	$215.22	$13,642.72
car loan	$363.32	$9,437.66
	Total Balance	$32,186.70

Monthly Payment for December, 2010

Department store	$64.53	$592.70
MasterCard	$106.94	$8,452.15
personal loan	$215.22	$13,563.93
car loan	$363.32	$9,145.12
	Total Balance	$31,753.90

Monthly Payment for January, 2011

Department store	$64.53	$538.54
MasterCard	$106.94	$8,443.82
personal loan	$215.22	$13,484.35
car loan	$363.32	$8,850.39
	Total Balance	$31,317.10

Monthly Payment for February, 2011

Department store	$64.53	$483.43
MasterCard	$106.94	$8,435.39
personal loan	$215.22	$13,403.97
car loan	$363.32	$8,553.45
	Total Balance	$30,876.24

Monthly Payment for
March, 2011

Department store	$64.53	$427.36
MasterCard	$106.94	$8,426.86
personal loan	$215.22	$13,322.79
car loan	$363.32	$8,254.28
	Total Balance	$30,431.29

Monthly Payment for
April, 2011

Department store	$64.53	$370.31
MasterCard	$106.94	$8,418.23
personal loan	$215.22	$13,240.80
car loan	$363.32	$7,952.87
	Total Balance	$29,982.21

Monthly Payment for
May, 2011

Department store	$64.53	$312.26
MasterCard	$106.94	$8,409.50
personal loan	$215.22	$13,157.99
car loan	$363.32	$7,649.20
	Total Balance	$29,528.95

Monthly Payment for
June, 2011

Department store	$64.53	$253.19

MasterCard	$106.94	$8,400.67	
personal loan	$215.22	$13,074.35	
car loan	$363.32	$7,343.25	
	Total Balance	$29,071.46	

Monthly Payment for July, 2011

Department store	$64.53	$193.09
MasterCard	$106.94	$8,391.74
personal loan	$215.22	$12,989.87
car loan	$363.32	$7,035.00
	Total Balance	$28,609.70

Monthly Payment for August, 2011

Department store	$64.53	$131.94
MasterCard	$106.94	$8,382.70
personal loan	$215.22	$12,904.55
car loan	$363.32	$6,724.44
	Total Balance	$28,143.63

Monthly Payment for September, 2011

Department store	$64.53	$69.72
MasterCard	$106.94	$8,373.56
personal loan	$215.22	$12,818.38
car loan	$363.32	$6,411.55
	Total Balance	$27,673.21

Monthly Payment for October, 2011

Department store	$64.53	$6.41
MasterCard	$106.94	$8,364.31
personal loan	$215.22	$12,731.34
car loan	$363.32	$6,096.32
	Total Balance	$27,198.38

Monthly Payment for November, 2011

			Final Department Store Payment
Department store	$6.52	$0.00	
MasterCard	$164.95	$8,296.94	
personal loan	$215.22	$12,643.43	

| car loan | $363.32 | $5,778.72 | |
| | Total Balance | $26,719.09 | |

Monthly Payment for
December, 2011

			Pay difference toward next higher interest loan
MasterCard	$171.47	$8,222.27	
personal loan	$215.22	$12,554.64	
car loan	$363.32	$5,458.74	
	Total Balance	$26,235.65	

Monthly Payment for
January, 2012

MasterCard	$171.47	$8,146.73
personal loan	$215.22	$12,464.97
car loan	$363.32	$5,136.36
	Total Balance	$25,748.06

Monthly Payment for
February, 2012

MasterCard	$171.47	$8,070.31
personal loan	$215.22	$12,374.40
car loan	$363.32	$4,811.56
	Total Balance	$25,256.27

Monthly Payment for
March, 2012

MasterCard	$171.47	$7,992.99
personal loan	$215.22	$12,282.92
car loan	$363.32	$4,484.33
	Total Balance	$24,760.24

Monthly Payment for
April, 2012

MasterCard	$171.47	$7,914.77
personal loan	$215.22	$12,190.53
car loan	$363.32	$4,154.64
	Total Balance	$24,259.94

Monthly Payment for
May, 2012

| MasterCard | $171.47 | $7,835.64 |
| personal loan | $215.22 | $12,097.22 |

car loan	$363.32	$3,822.48
	Total Balance	$23,755.34

Monthly Payment for
June, 2012

MasterCard	$171.47	$7,755.59
personal loan	$215.22	$12,002.97
car loan	$363.32	$3,487.83
	Total Balance	$23,246.39

Monthly Payment for July,
2012

MasterCard	$171.47	$7,674.60
personal loan	$215.22	$11,907.78
car loan	$363.32	$3,150.67
	Total Balance	$22,733.05

Monthly Payment for
August, 2012

MasterCard	$171.47	$7,592.67
personal loan	$215.22	$11,811.64
car loan	$363.32	$2,810.98
	Total Balance	$22,215.29

Monthly Payment for September, 2012

MasterCard	$171.47	$7,509.78
personal loan	$215.22	$11,714.54
car loan	$363.32	$2,468.74
	Total Balance	$21,693.06

Monthly Payment for
October, 2012

MasterCard	$171.47	$7,425.92
personal loan	$215.22	$11,616.47
car loan	$363.32	$2,123.94
	Total Balance	$21,166.33

Monthly Payment for
November, 2012

MasterCard	$171.47	$7,341.09
personal loan	$215.22	$11,517.41
car loan	$363.32	$1,776.55
	Total Balance	$20,635.05

Monthly Payment for
December, 2012

MasterCard	$171.47	$7,255.27
personal loan	$215.22	$11,417.36
car loan	$363.32	$1,426.55
	Total Balance	$20,099.18

Monthly Payment for
January, 2013

MasterCard	$171.47	$7,168.44
personal loan	$215.22	$11,316.31
car loan	$363.32	$1,073.93
	Total Balance	$19,558.68

Monthly Payment for
February, 2013

MasterCard	$171.47	$7,080.60
personal loan	$215.22	$11,214.25
car loan	$363.32	$718.66
	Total Balance	$19,013.51

Monthly Payment for
March, 2013

MasterCard	$171.47	$6,991.74
personal loan	$215.22	$11,111.17
car loan	$363.32	$360.73
	Total Balance	$18,463.64

Monthly Payment for
April, 2013

MasterCard	$171.47	$6,901.84
personal loan	$215.22	$11,007.06
car loan	$363.32	$0.12
	Total Balance	$17,909.02

Monthly Payment for
May, 2013

MasterCard	$534.67	$6,447.69
personal loan	$215.22	$10,901.91
car loan	$0.12	$0.00
	Total Balance	$17,349.60

Final car payment
put the Difference
toward the MC bill

Monthly Payment for
June, 2013

MasterCard	$534.79	$5,988.12
personal loan	$215.22	$10,795.71
	Total Balance	$16,783.83

Monthly Payment for July,
2013

MasterCard	$534.79	$5,523.19
personal loan	$215.22	$10,688.45
	Total Balance	$16,211.64

Monthly Payment for
August, 2013

MasterCard	$534.79	$5,052.84
personal loan	$215.22	$10,580.11
	Total Balance	$15,632.95

Monthly Payment for September, 2013

MasterCard	$534.79	$4,577.00
personal loan	$215.22	$10,470.69
	Total Balance	$15,047.69

Monthly Payment for
October, 2013

MasterCard	$534.79	$4,095.61
personal loan	$215.22	$10,360.18
	Total Balance	$14,455.79

Monthly Payment for
November, 2013

MasterCard	$534.79	$3,608.60
personal loan	$215.22	$10,248.56
	Total Balance	$13,857.16

Monthly Payment for
December, 2013

MasterCard	$534.79	$3,115.91
personal loan	$215.22	$10,135.83
	Total Balance	$13,251.74

Monthly Payment for
January, 2014

MasterCard	$534.79	$2,617.47
personal loan	$215.22	$10,021.97

	Total Balance	$12,639.44
Monthly Payment for February, 2014		
MasterCard	$534.79	$2,113.22
personal loan	$215.22	$9,906.97
	Total Balance	$12,020.19
Monthly Payment for March, 2014		
MasterCard	$534.79	$1,603.08
personal loan	$215.22	$9,790.82
	Total Balance	$11,393.90
Monthly Payment for April, 2014		
MasterCard	$534.79	$1,086.99
personal loan	$215.22	$9,673.51
	Total Balance	$10,760.50
Monthly Payment for May, 2014		
MasterCard	$534.79	$564.88
personal loan	$215.22	$9,555.03
	Total Balance	$10,119.91
Monthly Payment for June, 2014		
MasterCard	$534.79	$36.68
personal loan	$215.22	$9,435.36
	Total Balance	$9,472.04

Monthly Payment for July, 2014

Final MC Payment. Now pay all toward personal loan

MasterCard	$37.11	$0.00
personal loan	$712.90	$8,816.81
	Total Balance	$8,816.81
Monthly Payment for August, 2014		
personal loan	$750.01	$8,154.97
	Total Balance	$8,154.97

Monthly Payment for September, 2014

personal loan	$750.01	$7,486.51
	Total Balance	$7,486.51

Monthly Payment for
October, 2014

personal loan	$750.01	$6,811.37
	Total Balance	$6,811.37

Monthly Payment for
November, 2014

personal loan	$750.01	$6,129.47
	Total Balance	$6,129.47

Monthly Payment for
December, 2014

personal loan	$750.01	$5,440.75
	Total Balance	$5,440.75

Monthly Payment for
January, 2015

personal loan	$750.01	$4,745.15
	Total Balance	$4,745.15

Monthly Payment for
February, 2015

personal loan	$750.01	$4,042.59
	Total Balance	$4,042.59

Monthly Payment for
March, 2015

personal loan	$750.01	$3,333.01
	Total Balance	$3,333.01

Monthly Payment for
April, 2015

personal loan	$750.01	$2,616.33
	Total Balance	$2,616.33

Monthly Payment for
May, 2015

personal loan	$750.01	$1,892.48
	Total Balance	$1,892.48

Monthly Payment for
June, 2015

personal loan	$750.01	$1,161.39
	Total Balance	$1,161.39

Monthly Payment for July, 2015

personal loan	$750.01	$422.99
	Total Balance	$422.99

Monthly Payment for August, 2015

personal loan	$427.22	$0.00
You are debt free, congratulations!	Total Balance	$0.00

If you followed this example, then you paid off this debt in almost half the expected time and saved $17,195.57 in interest. Examine the chart and you will see that the extra $37.07 went to the highest-interest loan, the department store card, first. Then the December 2011 payment shows the department store card paid off and the payment that was previously going toward that debt now goes to the MasterCard debt. In May 2013, the car loan was paid off and that payment is then reassigned to the higher-interest loan, the MasterCard. Then the MasterCard is paid off in the August 2014 payment. The total $750 now goes toward the personal loan until that is paid off in August 2015, making you debt-free in 6 years instead of 20 years.

If your discipline has been true and steady then not only have you paid $39,336.07 in debts, but you have been putting away, in your untouchable account, 10% of your income. At this point, 6 years later, you have put aside about $27,000. You went from owing almost $40,000 in debt to having in savings about $27,000—and remember that $27,000 was how much you put aside and does not include interest earnings. With a modest interest of 4%, your $27,000 is now $30,458.46. Your total net worth swing from the negative to the positive was about $69,794. This was in just 6 years, and is about $10,000 a year!

In those six years, you may get an increase in income, a secondary income, or some other source, and you should put 20% of that increase or other source of income toward your debt as well. This will make you debt-free sooner. Of course 10% of that increase should go into your untouchable account.

It is important to realize that you must not add debts during this payoff time or you will defeat the purpose of the plan and may cause yourself to be in debt forever.

If you find that your minimum payments are already more than 20% of your income then you are already in big trouble. My father used to tell me that "*if you are in a hole then it is time to stop digging.*" If you are paying more than 20% of your monthly salary toward minimum payments then you are in a big hole and need to stop digging. You are probably borrowing your way into bigger debt or not paying your bills on time and heading for a definite disaster.

The choices for this problem are bankruptcy, renegotiation, or a credit counseling service—or simply make the payments as you see fit. Another choice is a loan to consolidate these debts. This can work, but remember to just take the amount you need to pay off the loans and still make that 20% payment toward your new consolidation loan.

The big mistake that so many make at this juncture is that they borrow the amount that the 20% payment will make. In other words, instead of borrowing the $40,000 they owe with a 20-year payment schedule of $310.00 at 7% interest, they borrow $95,000 with a 20-year payment schedule of about the $750 monthly payment. This will completely defeat the purpose.

If you need to consolidate, and if you can, you must only borrow the amount of money to pay your debts, no more. Then you take the 20% of your salary and pay that to the single loan. You will pay it off several years in advance of the scheduled final payment.

In this example, the $40,000 loan that had a 20-year payment schedule of $310 per month at an average 7% interest will be paid off in about 5 1/2 years with a payment of $750 per month. So if you choose a consolidation loan, keep to the discipline of the 20%. Remember, no more than 20% of your salary toward your debt payment ever and no less than 20% until you are debt-free. Do not borrow more than the amount you owe.

If you choose to just pay your debtors less, they may object to it but you must realize that you and your family are more important than a big corporation or local bank. They will not support you when you are retired and wishing that you had put some money away instead of paying your debts on time.

Now you must learn to live on 70% of your income. That 70% must cover all of your other expenses, including housing and taxes. The best way to truly learn to do this is with a *budget*.

Here is another one of those words again: budget! The thought of a budget is absolutely painful to most people. It is worse than trying to count calories for a diet. However, it is time for you to decide whether you want to truly live a life of financial freedom or to be tied down to your debts and bills forever.

This is a sample budget (fig 1) for a single-income household with a $45,000 salary using the debts from above. As you will see, it isn't pretty. The next scary word is *sacrifice*. In this budget you can clearly see that it is impossible to have anything extra. It may even be best for this person to share an apartment with someone and split their living expenses in order to have some extra money for entertainment.

If the person, in this example, was to sacrifice their privacy and split the expenses, they would surely be rewarded. In the example discussed earlier, they would have a savings of about $30,000 in six years and be debt-free.

I have a very rich uncle who has a net worth of over a million dollars. He had one of those professions that we all dream of. This is the profession that truly is the most envied. It allowed him to have about 3 months off every year. He had holidays and two 10-day vacations on top of his 3 months off. He was also often home early, about 4 o'clock every day. He was so lucky!

But how did this schoolteacher become a millionaire? As a single man, he simply didn't need to move away from his parents. He lived with them until he was in his thirties and then found a low-priced apartment within walking distance from his employing school. This was clearly a man who had the discipline to save, and he has the results to show for it.

The following is a tough budget to follow, but in time and with sacrifice and discipline you too will have all you need to survive. Use this budget as a sample to make your own. I have found several companies, including programs like Quicken or Money, that have complicated budget programs that may work for you. If you are good with Excel then this should be easy to duplicate. You can also find a blank budget if you go to the website www.25milliondollarmasterminds.com.

Fig. 1
Example Using $45,000 Single Earner Salary Using Single Status with 1 Deduction

	Gross Monthly Pay	$3,750.00
	Fed withholding	$457.00
	Social Security	$252.50
	Medicare	$54.38
	State (Pa for example)	$115.13
	SUI	$2.25
	total deductions	**$881.26**
	total take home	$2,868.74

Pay your self first	**$375.00**	
Debt Allocation 20%	$750.00	
Auto Loan	$363.32	
credit card	$106.94	
personal loan	$215.22	
department store card	$64.53	
Spendable Balance	$1,743.74	
Transportation	**$250.00**	
Insurance	$100.00	
Gas	$100.00	
Maintenance	$50.00	
Home	**$1,100.00**	
Mortgage or rent	$750.00	
Maintenance		
Insurance	$50.00	
Groceries/ household supplies	$200.00	
Real Estate Tax	$100.00	
Utilities	**$255.00**	
Phone bill	$50.00	
Cable/internet	$55.00	
Gas/electric	$125.00	
Water	$25.00	
Entertainment	**$28.74**	
Memberships		
Dining out	$0.00	
Events	$0.00	
Subscriptions	$0.00	
Movies	$20.00	
Music		
Hobbies		
other	$8.74	

Miscellaneous		$110.00
	Dry Cleaning	
	New Clothes	
	Donations	
	Child Care	
	Tuition	
	Pocket Money	$100.00
	Gifts	$10.00
Total left over		$0.00

You will notice that the first deduction after your payroll taxes is the payment to yourself. You must make this the priority always. As I have stated before, only YOU will take care of YOU, not the banks that you paid on time or the restaurants you frequented or the department store that you bought the big-screen TV from. You must put aside the 10% for YOU. Think about this: If you called your car loan company and said "I made all of my payments on time, will you give me some money for retirement or for an emergency?" Not only would they not give you any but they probably wouldn't even lend you any if you didn't have a job at retirement. So take care of yourself, not the bank, because the bank won't take care of you.

Now that the debts are paid off in full, the 20% becomes money to allocate into different places. Take 5% and increase your deposit into your untouchable account for a total of 15% a year going toward this account. The other 15% is truly up to you. One suggestion is to place 5% into another account that we will call the "fun money" account. This account will be the money used for fun, such as vacations or a major purchase like a new car or appliance. The other 10% can either be put into daily spending or for a specific objective such as a remodel of your kitchen or bathroom. You would have 3 accounts now. The first would be your untouchable account with 15% of your earnings, the next would be a fun money account with 5% of your earnings, and the last account with up to 10% of your earnings for a specific goal such as a car or remodel of your home.

To become one of the "others" you must have *discipline*, you must *sacrifice* and you must have a *budget*. Remember that you are in control of your destiny and your money. Make the right decisions and you will soon become one of the "others."

You will find that the first three months are the hardest and then it will get easier and easier. You will look at the balance of your debts going down and you will see the balance of your "untouchable" account going up. This is such a motivating feeling and will truly help you to succeed.

You will have pitfalls and things will get in the way. Recently my car needed a $700 repair. In the old days I would put that in my credit card and just "blended it in" with the rest of the payments. As an outside salesperson my car is needed for my job, so it had to be fixed. I must admit I felt guilty taking this money from my "untouchable account," but I believe this qualified as an emergency. More importantly, I did not stop putting the money in the account and, with interest, this account is growing quickly. As a bonus, I did not add to my debt, and that is a good feeling.

All disciplines take time to adapt to. If you have ever been on a diet or tried to stop smoking, you know that it takes each and every day of discipline to continue to reach your goals. Sometimes it is hard and others near impossible, but it *can* be done. You can do it; I have faith in your ability for discipline and you should also.

To summarize:
1. Pay yourself first by putting 10% away in an untouchable account.
2. Pay your debts by allocating 20%, no more or less, toward your debts until you are debt free.
3. Budget and sacrifice because only you can take care of you.

Now for my next set of lottery numbers.

Remember to read these out loud, please!

12 22 32 42 52 Powerball 11

Chapter 5

The Lottery

The LORD commanded my lord to give the land for an inheritance by lot to the children of Israel. (Numbers 36.2 NIV)

It is hard to trace the origin of the very first lottery. We do know, however, that the concept of the lottery goes back far into Biblical times. In the above Bible verse, God is commanding that the land of Israel be divided by lots among the people of Israel. In Greek mythology, it was a lottery that divided the universe between the sons of Kronos. Poseidon got the sea and Zeus became the ruler of the heavens while Hades got the "misty darkness."

Throughout time and literature, the lottery is used for such things as giving away land, money, or wealth. Sometimes it is used to pick "volunteers" to perform a brave deed, such as a soldier going on a difficult mission or into battle. In some stories the lottery was used to choose a virgin to be sacrificed to a dragon or other monster. Sometimes it was even used to solve disputes between people. The lottery comes in many different forms. It could be numbers or choosing the short straw or a random pick of a name in a hat.

The lottery in its monetary form has been used to raise funds for various necessities in different parts of the world. As early as 200 BC, The Hun Dynasty used a lottery to raise funds to build the Great Wall of China. 1 This game of chance was called Keno. Keno was used to fund the great wall and the war effort. Cheung Lung, who introduced the idea, was having trouble funding the war effort and found it difficult to get people to volunteer contributions. When a monetary prize was offered in exchange for a gamble of small amounts of money the war effort got underway.

Today we use the lottery proceeds much in the same way. They are used to fund government programs such as aid for the elderly or public education.

The lottery that most of us are familiar with is the one in which we buy a ticket for a dollar, pick numbers, and then hope that the numbers picked at random by the lottery drawing match ours. There is tremendous controversy on the subject of the lottery. The odds against winning are so unbelievably high that it has been claimed that you are more than ten times more likely to be struck by lightning than you are to win the lottery. 2 This legalized form of gambling has stirred up quite a controversy.

Some call it a tax on the poor. They claim that mostly the poor play the lottery for that 1 in 120,526,770 (the odds of winning the Powerball) chance to get rich. Some even call it the "suckers' tax." Recently there was a form of legislation that was trying to limit the winnings for those on government programs such as welfare or food stamps. The claim is that the people on these programs should not be spending the government money they receive to feed themselves and their families on lottery tickets. (Sounds like the Blood Money Rule needs to be applied here.)

The idea is to limit the winnings so that the recipients of these programs will be discouraged from playing. Apparently the government thought twice about this idea when they realized that they may be discouraging the majority of the players from buying tickets, therefore selling fewer tickets and making less profit.

In Illinois a few years back, there was a billboard that advertised lottery tickets with this slogan: "This could be your way out." This slogan alone shows that a government that counts on lottery sales had decided that discouraging the majority of players from buying lottery tickets has to be a bad idea.

Then there are others who complain that it is legalized government gambling that adds to society's other gambling problems. Gambling problems, like other overindulgences, can lead to catastrophic problems for people. Not only is the loss of money a problem but the symptoms of an addict are very destructive. The need to play or gamble can overpower some and cause them to make some very stupid decisions. Often in casinos, compulsive gamblers will leave their children with strangers, or even unsupervised, because no one under 21 is allowed in the casino area. Women have had their children put in foster care because of this behavior and rightly so. Can you imagine the child that becomes an adult growing up in that type of environment?

Of course, the biggest problem with winning the lottery is you may actually win!

Whenever I think of the lottery, I am reminded of the movie called *The Island*. This movie starts out making you believe the characters in the movie have survived a great holocaust. The characters believe they are trapped in a facility that is protecting them from the nuclear waste that has enveloped the Earth. In this facility, the characters are well taken care of. Everything from the perfect temperature to the perfect food to exercise and recreation is provided for them. Even their bodily fluids are monitored constantly to make sure that they are perfectly healthy. They are told that as the Earth clears away this nuclear waste, they will be the ones who are chosen to go into the world to live on The Island.

The Island, as they believe, is paradise. The Island is everyone's dream. It is perfection; it is the place where everything will be better. They will see trees and water and the sun. That's right, the real sun, not just the fluorescent artificial lighting systems. The Island is where it will all begin again for them. Everything will be perfect and wonderful. Paradise! Everyone in the facility wishes they could win the lottery and go to the island.

Whenever the lottery is drawn all of the residents of the facility are called to the giant monitor where the names are drawn for the next set of lottery winners. Oh, how lucky these winners are. They get to live on the Island, paradise at last! The unfortunate majorities are the ones who must go back to their regular lives in the artificial environment and wish for the next day where they might be the next picked to win the lottery and go to the island.

This movie has many social and political messages, but as the story goes on we soon realize that the characters in the movie are simply being used for organ harvesting: when they "win" the lottery they are killed so that their organs can be harvested for transplantation to the very rich in society. There is no Island and no paradise. In reality, the winners are truly the losers.

So, why do I think of this movie? Well, how many stories have you heard about the people who actually win the lottery? If you search the Internet for stories of winners of the lottery, many of then will discuss how the winners' lives were ruined by winning the lottery.

So far this book has discussed rules of money, how to save it, how to keep it, and how to budget it. Now imagine that you are the $45,000-a-year earner who, in the last chapter, actually started to practice discipline and sacrifice. Imagine now if you held the lottery ticket that was in fact the winner of $25,000,000—and not just $25,000,000, but a $25,000,000 cash payout after taxes. What would you do?

Here it is: the big question that needs big answers. Casually ask people whom you know what they would do if they won $25,000,000 in the lottery and you will get similar answers. "I would quit my job." "I would move to an island." I would buy an island." "I would drive a big car." "I would have a limo driver drive my big car." "I would party all night long." These are just some of the answers you would get. The fact is none of these answers truly have any substance. Some may even tell you that they would be happy, eternally happy. Well read some of these stories I found on a search of the Internet of people who won the lottery.

According to an article on the internet by Ellen Goodstein from Bankrate. com: 3

> "Winning the lottery isn't always what it's cracked up to be," says Evelyn Adams, who won the New Jersey lottery not just once, but twice (1985, 1986), to the tune of $5.4 million. Today the money is all gone and Adams lives in a trailer.
>
> "I won the American dream but I lost it, too. It was a very hard fall. It's called rock bottom," says Adams.
>
> "Everybody wanted my money. Everybody had their hand out. I never learned one simple word in the English language -- 'No.' I wish I had the chance to do it all over again. I'd be much smarter about it now," says Adams, who also lost money at the slot machines in Atlantic City.

This woman won the lottery twice and is now broke. She is actually living in a trailer.

Another man in the article states that he won $16.2 Million and is now on food stamps and living off social security of $450 a month. Another woman won $4.2 million and is now in debt and wishes she could win the lottery again so that she could get herself out of debt!

Other stories are those of greed and total irresponsibility that lead to lawsuits, murder, and suicide. Imagine killing yourself because you won the lottery!

There is a great literary work by John Steinbeck called *The Pearl*. In this story the main character is named Kino. Kino lives with his wife, Juana, and infant child Coyotito. They live in a very poor fishing village. The book starts out describing how everyone in the village wishes they could find a pearl that will make their lives perfect and wonderful. As the story goes on Kino finds a pearl. Not just a pearl, but the biggest pearl anyone has ever seen or heard of.

If you have read the book then you know that the lives of Kino, Juana and their son Coyotito are ruined by this find. Everyone in the village wants a piece of the pearl's riches. Some even try to convince Kino that the pearl is not very valuable and try to buy it for a fraction of its true value. The evil thoughts of the townspeople cause some to conspire to steal it. Then the most tragic thing of all happens: Coyotito, the infant child, gets killed when someone tries to steal the pearl.

Finally the couple realizes that the pearl has brought them nothing but fear, greed, and heartache, so they throw the pearl back into the ocean.

It is interesting that Steinbeck used the name Kino for his character in this book. You should have already made the connection to the name of the Chinese lottery, Keno.

So far the highest lottery-winning tragedy has to be that of Jack Whittaker who won $315 million dollars. 4 He has truly lived the story of Steinbeck's *The Pearl*. His euphoria of wining had him giving money away like a madman. He helped his local church build a new building and opened a foundation where people could ask for money. He was getting requests for all types of crazy things. He got requests for cars and houses and entertainment systems. He actually gave away over 50 million dollars of gifts to strangers. People would actually walk up to him in the street and ask for money.

Like in the Steinbeck story, he lost his granddaughter to the money. She became a drug addict and was mysteriously killed. She was his pride and joy and now she is gone. Mr. Whittaker started drinking heavily and didn't care much about anything. He would even have fistfights in bars in a drunken rage. Mr. Whittaker actually calls the lottery a "curse."

This was a successful businessman who was doing quite well when the onslaught of all this money derailed him from true success in his family and in his business. A very sad story indeed, and it would benefit many lottery winners to read stories like this before they go and cash in that lottery ticket.

The other problem is that there are so many other ways of winning the lottery. Some are literal versions of the lottery, yet some are the once-in-a-lifetime chance of doing something that brings someone great riches.

Have you heard of stories of people getting rich in other ways? They can be sports figures, singers, actors. The popular television show *American Idol* is a perfect example of another way to "win the lottery." Thousands come out to audition (and frankly some shouldn't), but in the end there is only one winner for each season.

During the first year of the show, the advertisements for contestants stated that the winner would win a million dollar recording contract. Of course now the world knows that this lottery of talent is worth several million dollars to winners and the money does not need to be mentioned any longer.

What about an inventor or a businessman with a once-in-a-lifetime idea who makes millions either marketing or selling the idea to someone else? Steve Jobs or Bill Gates certainly had no idea that they would be among the richest people in the world when they were tinkering with computers. Or maybe someone just truly excels at their profession or gets lucky when the company they work for gets sold and the stocks options that were a nice little perk become worth millions. There are so many ways that people can metaphorically "win the lottery."

So what will it be? Will you be the next winner and meet with the same fate of some of these famous people?

These are just some of the many famous people who have filed for bankruptcy: Susan Powter, Randy Quaid, Burt Reynolds, Mickey Rooney,

Dee Snider, Lawrence Taylor, Mark Twain, Mike Tyson, Gary Coleman, and several others. This just proves that no one is immune to the problems that come with quick and instant riches.

There are so many stories of people getting rich literally overnight... and then broke just several years later. And not just broke: some of them are living in poverty and ruin with no hope. They are far worse off than they were before they "won the lottery." I would think that these famous people, just like those living in the tent cities described earlier in this book, wish they'd had a plan while they had the money.

So what is the real problem? It is very simple, but extremely complicated. Everyone wants to be rich, but no one thinks about the things they want or want to do when they get there. I remember an interview with Evil Knievel in which he stated that he could easily spend a million dollars in a day. This was an interview after Evil had already filed for bankruptcy a few years earlier.

The problem with theses stories and the people in them is the fact that they had millions and they were all famous. Take a minute to think about what you would do if you won only a small amount in the lottery, say $50,000 after taxes. What would you do with it? You might pay debts, buy a car, throw a party, give some away, put a deposit on a house, or maybe save it. The question is, how long would you have it for? The answer in most cases is not very long.

Sure, with a $50,000 windfall, many would have a great story to tell about how they quickly spent the money—but after it was gone, it would be gone forever.

So now you might be starting to think about what you would do with a lottery winning or a windfall to keep you out of trouble and in control. That is the first part of what this book is truly about.

Personally, I want to win the lottery and I believe that one day I will. I am not sure if it will be the Powerball or another metaphoric type but I will win!

To help me, I again ask that you read my lottery numbers out loud.

My next set of lottery numbers:

Remember, please read them out loud.

11 15 30 42 48 Powerball 11

Chapter 6

My $25,000,000

I am not one of those who watches the numbers get picked on television. I usually read them the next day in an e-mail from the lottery commission or go to my local 7-Eleven, where I buy my tickets. I check them on the ticket scanner, which is the newest and coolest tool for the lazy lottery player like me. You simply put your ticket up to the reader and voilà, it displays whether you are a winner or not.

So one day, I will wake up and look at the numbers in the e-mail, or check the scanner at the convenience store, and there they will be! My numbers! The numbers I play every week. The numbers that I picked one day, thinking, "These are the ones." The numbers that are printed in this book, the numbers that you have been reading out loud, the numbers that will let me stand in front of the camera at the lottery commission holding that big check while they take my picture. The numbers that will give me a $25,000,000 lump sum after taxes!

So how will I handle it? Will I be broke in a few years? Will my family hate me? Will I put a family member into business and then need to keep giving them money because they are terrible at business? Will I be living in a trailer in 10 years? Will I waste it all on parties and other meaningless items? Will I wish I had never won the lottery in the first place? Will I feel it was a curse?

Well, here are some stories of the people who didn't change much after a big winning in the lottery. A man from Troy, NY won $65 million in the lottery and states, according to the article on the Lottery Post website, that his life is pretty much the same as it was before. He simply feels more financially secure.[1] He didn't waste it all or lose it all or give it away. He kept it and kept his life just the same.

Most of us dream of the toys we would buy, and believe me, I will list a few, but to Jim Hall, his biggest toy after the $65 million dollar winnings was a PT cruiser convertible and a Chrysler Prowler. The Halls live a simple but secure life on a ranch with some horses. One of the best comments made in the article at lotterypost.com was how they handle the telemarketers who want a piece of the money. To put it simply, no telemarketer can withstand the tongue-lashing they get from Mr. Hall.[1]

Brad Duke, according to several posted articles on the Internet, was also one of those people who is also very happy and very smart with his winnings. [2] Brad won $85 million and his goal is to turn it into $1 billion. He has assembled a team of top-notch financial advisors who are helping him reach his goals. He was very smart about giving his money away. He didn't!

It appears that most of the problems that the winners encounter are the greedy hands of family, friends, and beggars who want the lottery winnings. There are several studies about how lottery winners tend to give the money away to friends, family, and other organizations. I often wonder if any of the family members who received such offerings are now richer than the actual winner. I would imagine there is a lot of guilt associated with winning a lottery of millions. The guilt of not deserving it, the guilt of the needy people in the world, or the guilt of pulling up to a family member's house with your new Mercedes and seeing the old beat-up car in the driveway that your brother drives to work every day. Maybe even the guilt of your brother or sister's house being too small for his or her family.

Well, Brad's answer is simple: he created a family foundation in which he donates $12,000 a year to his selected family members. I hope his family members appreciate it, but if they don't appreciate it and they feel they deserve more, too bad! I applaud Brad for his loyalty and discipline. If you remember the rules of money then you will remember that "blood money" is often the ruin of many families.

When I started to think about writing this book, I asked several people what they would do if they won $25,000,000 in the lottery, and as I stated before, most gave pretty vague answers. When I asked my mother, her answer was all about generosity for her children. I hope she won't be insulted by me discussing this in this book, but I thought it was appropriate.

Her answer was something like this: she would take $7 million to live on and give the rest to her children. Each child, my 2 brothers and I, would receive $4 million, with no rules or limits. Her grandchildren, who to this date are 6 in total, would receive the rest in trust until they were old enough to need the money. She had it all planned out in about 5 minutes. Well Mom, I hope you win; I would love to have the $4 million. That is, of course, if I don't win my own $25,000,000 first!

The conversation then took an interesting turn when she asked me what I would do if I won $25 million. She specifically wanted to know how much I would give her. When I told her I wasn't ready to reveal that yet, well, she started to get upset. She then said "I hope you will at least give your *mother* a million dollars!"

Needless to say I was very surprised at her anger that was brewing under the surface. I sort of felt a piece of the pressure that lottery winners must feel when they win. I didn't even have a winning ticket and my mother was making me feel guilty about not promising her a million dollars if I won $25 million. I wonder if she felt I should also give my brothers a million each, and what about my children, would she guilt me into giving them a million each also? I finally agreed that if I won $25 million, I would buy her a house in Florida. I am not sure but I think that satisfied her for now.

So how will I avoid the traps of the lottery winner that will make me more miserable or feel cursed? How do I avoid living in a trailer only a few years after winning the lottery? What will I do with the winnings?

Before I get to the actual break down, I took the time to evaluate the type of person I am. This is an exercise that everyone should think about often. Not only the type of person you are, or I am, but what things truly make us happy. I will explain more of this type of thinking in a future chapter, but first I want to tell you a little about myself.

At the time of writing this, I have pretty much nothing as far as assets. If I were to list them, they would consist of: a motorcycle (Harley Davidson Electro-Glide), an automobile worth about $12,000 on which I owe about $9000, a few computers from my last failed business, and some jewelry worth about $2000 at best. Of course I also have a 50-inch Plasma TV and various pieces of furniture.

You see, I have been up and down with money several times in my life. I am currently losing my house to foreclosure and last year I filed for bankruptcy. My current credit score is about 450 points and I have a tax lien on my credit report as well. It sounds horrible, doesn't it? So how did I get here? Well, it started a long, long time ago in a place far, far away…:

Brooklyn, NY.

I remember being a kid growing up in Brooklyn, and I remember each birthday I would wish for the same thing as I blew out the candles on my birthday cake: a million dollars!

Little did I know at the time that I would, in the future, have this "million dollars." Unfortunately, like most people, I didn't know what that meant, what to do with a million dollars, nor how to keep it.

I have always been extremely enterprising. When I was just 11 or 12, I started installing car stereos in the parking lot of the local radio store.

Somehow, I had convinced the store manager that his sales would increase if he offered installation. The manager took a big risk but allowed me to install the various electronics, such as stereos and CB radios, in the customers' cars. I remember working for hours in the parking lot to make a mere $20-$30 on each job. It wasn't much, but I was a young kid who liked to spend money and now I had some to spend.

Spending money: that is the problem. I spent my money, and this bad habit of spending is mostly why my asset list reads as it does even today. I have, of course, started the disciplines laid out in the earlier chapters and I am moving away from spending it all. But let me not regress, as I want you to learn more of who I am and how I got myself into the predicament I am in today.

I continued being enterprising and mostly made money as a kid doing various kinds of electronics work. After high school, I tried to go to college but the combination of my parents getting divorced and my ambition to move ahead had me drop out in my first year. I landed a job in an arcade and was in charge of the maintenance and repairs of the pinball machines. Now, it is important to know that I was now 18 years old and had never had any experience in repairing pinball machines, but I had a desire to learn and I learned quickly. My experience in electronics led me to go to work for an electronics retailer. There I repaired the various televisions, stereos, VCRs, etc. I remember that on my first day I had no idea what I was doing, but again I simply had the desire to do it and eventually did it very well.

After a while I started to admire the salespeople on the floor and heard about the commissions and sales incentives called "spiffs" that they were earning. I thought about how I would like to try that. Well, within a few months, I was one of the top salespeople in the company and was made a manger of one of the stores.

I stuck with retail sales for a while and found that the thing I enjoyed the most was training other salespeople. At one of the stores I had worked for, I would hold a weekly sales training class. Several of the salespeople who attended this class would find that they would try the techniques I would teach and truly increase their sales and commissions.

Next was insurance sales; I often tell others that if you want to learn to sell anything, learn by selling life insurance. Life insurance is truly something that people have to be sold. Most people do not just wake up one day and say, "I think I will buy life insurance today." As a matter of fact, when someone would call in unsolicited, we would ask, "What is wrong with you, are you sick or dying?" Okay maybe that is an exaggeration, but sure enough they were always harder to get through underwriting because we knew something was wrong if they called us before we called them.

Life insurance sales combines all of the true techniques of sales: everything from cold calling to closing techniques. I enjoyed learning these techniques and some day I hope to write about these and the other interesting sales techniques I have learned.

After a divorce from my first wife I moved on to newer ventures, and after a few misguided career moves I learned about the computer consulting business. I managed to get a job selling for a medium-sized consulting firm. I truly excelled at this business and found it to be fun and exciting. I was making commissions well into the $200,000 range, plus a small salary and expenses. This was truly a dream job with a great income for 1997.

I then decided to open my own firm a few years later. Now I was married to my second wife and things looked good. I bought a few income-producing real estate properties and was making some serious money. I was building equity in the houses that I was renting, and business was good, so I decided to expand. The home we owned was worth about $700,000 at the time and things were looking great. We had the American dream: a beautiful home, money in good solid investments, and a pretty normal life.

On September 1st, 2001, I closed on the purchase of a competitor who had two large projects that I thought I could make some money with. Both of these projects were airline-related contracts. 10 days later the world changed when hijackers flew planes into the World Trade Center and the Pentagon. Three months later I closed the doors forever.

Unfortunately, not only did the 9/11 disaster close my business, but I have to admit that it affected me mentally as well. Many people had a sort of 9/11 "shell shock" and I was truly one of them. For months after the event, I saw the pictures at the local train station of the missing. The media would continue to play the footage, and the developing stories of the anthrax mail attacks a few months later would continue.

All of this had an effect on many of us and truly affected me in ways I could not verbalize. I had to sell the rental properties to cover the outstanding loans on the business and was struggling to find a job. I came to the realization that I was no longer the owner of a great business.

They say that every man goes through a mid-life crisis at one point or another. Some men buy Corvettes or other symbols of the youth they lost. Some have affairs and some leave their families, or change careers, or do some stupid things they will regret in the future. It was about a month after I closed the business, and about three months after the 9/11, attacks when I reached the final straw.

I had a great pain in the left side of my abdomen. It is funny how when you have a pain that you only think you should go to the hospital for, you probably didn't need to go, but when you have a pain that you *know* you need to go the hospital for, you go quickly!

I was admitted to the hospital and they found that my spleen had ruptured spontaneously. After an operation that held me in the hospital to recover for two weeks, and then six more weeks of recovering at home, I received a phone call from the hospital confirming the cause of spleen rupture. It was caused by a rare genetic disease called Gaucher's disease. This is a disease that, simply put, eats away at organs and bones. It is basically a genetic disorder that prevents the body from producing an enzyme that breaks up a fatty substance. This fatty substance, if not broken up and excreted, will build up and basically replace the cells of bones and organs in the body. This will lead to bone pain, bone weakness, broken bones, and organ failure if not treated.

The good news is that there is a treatment. This treatment consists of a replacement therapy of the enzyme through an intravenous infusion every two weeks. The cost is about half a million dollars a year and that does not include the battery of tests every year to be sure it is working.

So here it is: I've lost my business, the 9/11 disaster is still fresh in my mind, I am out of work, selling my properties to pay off the bank loans, and I am diagnosed with the genetic disorder. If there was ever a perfect storm for mid-life crises, I had found it. This is what led to the spiral downtown that follows.

My next crazy idea was to own a bed and breakfast on a large piece of land and do woodworking. I had assumed that if I was successful at the computer consulting business, then I would also be successful at running a B&B. Well, I never stood a chance. I didn't examine the books well enough and didn't have the backing I needed to stay afloat. My mid-life crisis was also playing tricks on my mind and this idea of the B&B ended in the divorce of my second wife and the sale of the property.

Having no business nor a job, I decided to sell real estate. Now this is about the year 2005 and the market is red hot. Not only am I a good salesman, I also understand rental properties. I decided to niche market myself as the investment property expert. After all, I had built up quite a few rental properties before and did very well with them. I started to sell investment properties using the technique of hosting seminars. These seminars were geared to people interested in buying properties. I even produced a DVD with my seminar for those who couldn't make the actual seminar.

I then decided to leverage some of my properties to buy other properties. I stopped following my own cash-flow rules. I started to get greedy, because everyone was making money by buying properties and selling them a few months later for large profits. This lasted about two more years, and then the financial bottom of the world dropped out. Remember the first chapter all about the spending and leveraging frenzy? Well, I would consider myself one of those people who leveraged it all and lost it all.

So here it is, a recap of where I am now. I have lost all of my rental properties and my principal residence to foreclosure. My credit score is about 450 and I own nothing but a motorcycle and a car that I owe money to the bank for. I have also filed for bankruptcy and it has been discharged. I live with my third wife-to-be, and the most wonderful person I have ever met, my girlfriend Carol. I have a job that I started about 5 months ago, and I make about $60,000 a year. That is my life at the time of writing this book. Now, where was I? Oh yeah, the lottery.

Now to get back to the topic; as I said, I will probably look at the lottery numbers that are e-mailed to me or scan the tickets at the convenience store the morning after the lottery numbers are drawn. I will examine the Powerball number first to see if it matches my Powerball pick. If it does I will then look at the other numbers and examine them one by one. I am sure that I will look at the winning ticket several times in total disbelief. My heart will race and the excitement will bubble up within me. I will probably let out a scream that resembles a teenage girl seeing the Beatles on the Ed Sullivan show in the 1960's.

"HOLY CRAP I WON! YEEEESSSSSSS!"

So what will I do next?

There are several suggestions on the Internet that suggest you keep your identity a secret. Frankly, I am not sure if that is what I will do. I will contact my lawyer to be sure that I remain safe from the people who want handouts, but the purpose of this chapter is to outline how I will allocate and spend the $25 million, so here it is....

First, a recap of the clichés/rules of money.

"Stretch a dollar."

"A penny saved is a penny earned."

"Put your money where your mouth is."

"Money doesn't grow on trees."

"There's gold in them thar hills."

"Money is burning a hole in my pocket."

"Penny wise and pound foolish."

"Blood money."

"Money is the root of all evil."

As I spend this money I intend to be mindful of the rules of money, so here it goes.

The following assumes a $25 million cash payout after all taxes.

If you recall, in the last chapter my personal rules stated that ½ of all unexpected money goes into the untouchable account. This will be one of my safety nets to keep money from **burning a hole in my pocket**. I will probably divide this $12.5 million into 4 different accounts with 4 different risk levels. The first will be a cash equivalent risk that will be something like a CD in a bank. I will take a long term CD for probably five or ten years and leave the money in that account. The next will be a moderate speculation account that will be a fund of equity type investments, the third part will go into a riskier growth fund such as a hedge fund, and the last quarter will go into my regular stocks trading account that allows me to trade stocks and options on my own. The latter is the most risky but also the most fun.

Here is a smart plan for the accounts: I have allocated $12.5 million for all 4 accounts, which means that $4.125 million will go into each fund. I will pick three separate brokers for each of the 3 funds and a separate company for the trading account. The reason for the 3 brokers is for balance. I am sure to get several opinions from each of the brokers and that will allow me to make better decisions.

Another important reason for the separate brokers is that many times the representative or salesperson will leave that brokerage or leave the business completely. They may retire or move away or even get ill and be forced out of the business. I do not want to rely on the person who inherits my orphaned fund. I want to be sure that at least 2/3s of my advisory team is still in place. That way, I am assured that my team will continue to know my original goals and desires.

And yet another reason to use separate brokers is apparent when you think about many of the brokerages and hedge fund managers that turned out to be stealing their clients' money. I would hate to win the lottery and find out that I gave all the money to someone like Bernie Madoff to invest it for me. So, that's the first $12.5 million accounted for.

Now I will have $12.5 million to continue with. Another cliché to follow is that **money does not grow on trees**, so I will need an income to live comfortably with my bride-to-be (or bride, if I win after we are married). I feel that an income of $250,000 will be sufficient for the lifestyle we will want to have. That means an annuity. I will again pick four different annuity companies for the same reason as above. Another good reason for the four annuity companies is that I can get each annuity to pay monthly, on a different week of the month, so that I will get a weekly income. The amount of money needed with today's income annuity to produce $250,000 a year is about 4 million dollars.

There are many websites and annuity brokers that can give you this type of information, and I have researched it thoroughly. I found that they pay the owner until his or her death. The difference in annuities is that they change with the type of beneficiary arrangement. I will be sure to get one that pays Carol, my bride-to-be, a continued $250,000 a year for the rest of her life if I should die before her. That leaves $8.5 million to spend, give away, and have a little fun with.

So you must think that the first 2/3s of the winnings was pretty boring, but if it isn't put aside and if income isn't generated then eventually the money will be gone with no way to replace it. The $250,000 a year for life guarantees me a decent or substantial salary to live on. The $12.5 million put aside ensures that if I truly want something special in the future or need something, then I have a secure place to take some money from. Also, that money will be making me money and working hard every minute of every day for me. As discussed, some of the money will be invested in low risk funds with low returns and some at high risk with the possibility of high returns. This makes **a penny saved, a penny earned**.

Now, the fun of the rest of the money....

$8.5 million to spend: first a home that Carol and I will want to have for the rest of our prime years together. I believe $1,000,000 will cover that home, including all closing costs. We are older and none of our children live with us. That means a 3 bedroom home with a 3-4 car garage. The large garage will hold the cars and motorcycles. Both of us like to ride motorcycles and should have a couple of different bikes in the future, but I will get to that.

The home will be in Bucks County, PA, where we live now, probably in the New Hope or Washington's Crossing area. Although we both eventually want to live near water (I prefer Maui and she prefers something like Florida or California), we still have children in the area so we will continue to have roots here for a while. We will probably sell the home in the future and move to a warmer destination.

Now for the giveaways and gifts. The giveaways to our children will be as follows: each will receive $100,000.00 immediately. That's right, just one hundred thousand. If you have read the past chapter then you know what happens to people who have money thrown at them too fast. I truly believe that I will hurt my children more by giving them too much, too fast, so that is all they get for now. Sorry, Mom.

My two brothers will also receive the same $100,000 gift immediately. Carol's sister and daughter will also receive the $100,000 gift. My mother and father will also receive the $100,000 gift (my mother is supposed to be getting a house in Florida as well, if you recall, but we will get to that shortly). That is a total of $1,000,000 gifted to family immediately.

A list of charities will receive another million spilt between them. I will have a charity for children and families who suffer from autism that $100,000 will fund. Our local church and place of worship will receive a grant to do something special with up to $250,000. The rest of the million will be given to a company that specializes in raising money for smaller charities. I will turn to a company like <u>ProFundraisers.com</u>. People like Steve Forbus, the owner of this company, will be in charge of which organization needs the money the most and how to distribute it. That way if I receive the phone calls from begging charities, I can send these people to Steve and let him handle it, avoiding the guilt of turning people down.

Only $5.5 million left!

Now for the cars and motorcycles! Almost a million dollars' worth will be bought for me, Carol, and our kids. My car will be the Cadillac XLR-V Convertible. This sells for about $100,000. Carol wants the Mercedes equivalent SL550 Roadster for about $100,000. Our everyday car will be our 4-seater coupe, the BMW 750i, also for about $100,000. Each of the boys will receive a Mustang GT convertible of the color of their choice. Two boys equals about $80.000 total for these cars. The girls, between Carol and me, are a total of 3, and will also receive cars of their choosing for about the same $40,000 price tag. I also promised my younger brother, Seth, an Infiniti G37 for about $40,000. My other brother will also get the car of his liking for about the same price tag, and Carol's sister will receive one as well. I have a friend who recently had a stroke and needs a van for him and his wife to get around. I will buy them a van for about $30,000. That is a total of $650,000 worth of cars.

I should also explain that the order in which I am writing this list may not be the exact order in which I will spend the money. For example, the day I look at the winning numbers on my computer and realize that I won will be a hard day for me to keep quiet, but I will try. My intention is to surprise my love Carol with a Harley Davidson Cross-Bones motorcycle. This is her dream bike. I would like her to pull up to our quaint townhouse and see it in the driveway before I tell her, "WE WON!"

The motorcycle with all the accessories will be about $22,000. I also want another motorcycle which will probably be a Harley Davidson Screaming Eagle Dyna for about $30,000. One of my dreams is to have a custom bike made by the Tuetels on American Chopper, but I think I will wait for that one, although a "Lottery Bike" might be an interesting theme.

Next is the Fiji island party (and wedding if Carol and I are not yet married). I intend to fly my closest friends and family to the Fiji Islands for a week. There is a resort that for $500,000/week you can have the island to yourself and your guests. The plane fare and all the other accommodations will come to about $250,000. I think it is important to treat your friends to something special and I also think it may keep the jealousy at bay. I truly believe my friends will appreciate this gesture and I hope and believe that they will not feel it is an entitlement because they know a lottery winner.

Whoa, that still leaves about $4 million! New furniture for the new house will be about $150,000, landscaping will be about $100,000 and redecorating should be in the range of $100,000 as well.

Now for the house in Florida! This will be the expensive piece. A compound with a house and a smaller guest house for my family and friends to stay whenever they want. This is how I will solve the promise of the house in Florida to my mother. I hope she appreciates it. The house will be on the water with a boat dock. (I haven't told you about the boat yet; that is next.) The house should cost about $1.7 million, and about $300,000 for furniture landscaping and improvements will probably do just fine. The house will have a grand entrance with a paved driveway and 3 to 4 garages for the cars and motorcycles. West Palm Beach puts us close to friends and relatives, so that will be the perfect location.

The boat will be a sailboat. So far I like the Beneteau brand. The 42' to 47' boats run used for about $275,000. Sailing has been a dream of mine for a long time. I will probably need about $25,000 for all the accessories for the boat for a total of $300,000.

Now I have about $1.5 million left. Time to splurge! Jewelry, watches, clothes, etc. This should be a day or a week of just spending to get it out of our system. Take a half million and just spend like it is "going out of style." A Rolex watch for me, a beautiful necklace for Carol, gold and diamond rings for both of us. Expensive restaurants, a Broadway play or two, Armani suits and dresses; just spend for a day or a week to get it out of our system and frankly to have some fun.

There was a movie, which Richard Pryor starred in, called *Brewster's Millions*. This was the story of a man who was to inherit $30 million dollars. Because his long-lost relative felt that it was too much money for Brewster to inherit all at once, he gave Brewster a test. The test was to spend 3 million dollars in 30 days. Although the movie was a comedy, I believe the premise should be admired and taken seriously to avoid the "money burning a hole in your pocket" problems that may occur if a money spending spree is not taken advantage of. In the movie, the main character Brewster actually got tired of trying to spend the $3 million. It became difficult and burdensome, but he did it. For me a limit of about $500,000 will need to be strictly adhered to. This limit will also help with the discipline needed to keep money.

So now about $1,000,000 is left over. I think a money market checking account for discretionary spending will do for this million. I am sure that

I forgot something or someone that I may need this for. That's it for my $25,000,000. It is all well planned out.

Here is a recap of the money:

- $12.5 million in untouchable accounts split into 4 separate risk categories, including the highest risk, a stock trading account.
- $4 million dollars into 4 separate annuity accounts for a total of $250,000 income per year. Remember that property taxes, utilities, boat docking fees and other costs including basic living expenses will come with this lifestyle, so this income will be needed to cover these costs.
- $1 million for a house in Bucks County. This will be a temporary house for the next 7-10 years, but it will be well kept on at least 2 acres. I estimate about $350,000 for furniture, landscaping, etc.
- $1 million in total gifts to the children, our siblings, and my parents of $100,000 each. I will probably give them more in the future from the untouchable account. For example, a gift of $10,000 a year for a birthday present would be appropriate. I may also pay for a special occasion like a wedding as it comes up. The intention is not to take away their drive to work or to earn for themselves by feeling they can tap into the lottery fortune when they need to.
- $1,000,000 for various charities. I will have a charity fundraising company control to keep me protected from the solicitations.
- $750,000 for new cars for the siblings, the children, and a gift for a friend, plus our special cars and motorcycles.
- $2 million on a waterfront property in West Palm Beach with a guest house for our friends and relatives. Included in that is the cost of all of the decorating and furniture.
- $300,000 for the sail boat to dock next to the house. About a 42' to 47' foot boat.
- $750,000 party for my friends and relatives (or wedding, if Carol and I are not yet married).
- $500,000 spending spree, just for fun.
- $1 million approximately left over for things I may have forgotten or the might-as-wells. The might-as-wells are those things you buy when are buying something else and say "I might as well get this also."

So there you have it: $25,000,000 accounted for. If you have been thinking about what you would do with your winnings, hold that thought; we will get to it.

Now, once again, here is my next set of lottery numbers.

Remember, please read them out loud!

14 21 23 25 41 Powerball 11

Chapter 7

I forgot to buy my ticket!

An old joke:

Father John would pray every day for the same thing. "God, please let me win the lottery today." 10 years passed and Father John was praying now with the same words, again and again, "God, please let me win the lottery today." 20 years passed with the same prayer, "God, please let me win the lottery today." After 30 years of prayer and no results, Father John looked up and said, "God, I have been praying for 30 years and I still have not won the lottery! Why aren't you answering my prayers?" Then Father John heard a loud voice say, "If you would just buy one ticket!"

The odds of winning the lottery are 1 in 195,249,054. Yet even with those odds, some people continue to think that this is the only way for them to get rich. There must be other ways to make money besides winning the lottery. After all, there are several millionaires, even billionaires, who never bought a lottery ticket. I am not just talking about earning a living or not struggling through each day, I am talking about a large sum of money or a continual large income. Why is it that some people have it and some people don't? What makes the people who have it different?

In chapters 3 and 4, I discussed the rules of money and how to keep it. Certainly this is a start in the right direction and these lessons will help everyone live a better financial life for a long time. If you learn nothing more from this book, those lessons along with a balanced budget will be the path to truly not worrying about your financial situation. Yet, if you truly want it, there is more.

The question is, how can we get all the money we want, without winning the lottery?

The answer is in the magic of *desire*. Desire is truly the route to riches. Desire is one of the most powerful forces in the all the world. Yes, you can truly think your way to where you want to be. If you desire a million dollars, you will have it. If you desire a new car, let's say a Mercedes, you again will have it. If you desire a new house or a second house by the beach, you will truly have it. Even if you desire to be President, you can do it.

So right now you are reading this and you are thinking about how you need something right now. It may be money, it may be a material item, or maybe it is a new job or a promotion, and you are thinking, why don't I have it right now, I want it now!

It is important to understand that the difference between wanting and desiring is huge. We all want a million dollars, but to desire a million dollars takes effort. Of course it takes the effort of working towards it, but it also takes the effort of thinking about it, about how you are going to get it and what you are going to do with it. Desire is a thought process and a deep-down want of something, not an emergency thought like, "I wish I had the $600 for tires for my car."

This is truly the difference between those who have it and those who don't. Currently the most famous person who desired something and obtained it is President Barrack Obama. It makes no difference what your political views are; you must admire his desire and achievements. With so many odds against him, like his race, his name, and his birthplace to name a few, he not only won the Democratic nomination but became our 44th president.

If you watch some of the speeches that he gave during his campaign for the Presidency, you can clearly see his desire and determination. It was clear that in his mind, he had already won. If you look at some of the footage of his Democratic competitor, Hillary Clinton, it was also clear that she was not sure if could win—or maybe, deep down, she knew she didn't want to. Clearly her speeches and mannerisms did NOT say "I desire to be President."

Even a few days before the actual Presidential vote, John McCain, the competitor, was saying how he felt Obama would make a good President and America had nothing to fear by electing him. Some say that McCain conceded right there, at that moment. Barack Obama, with his desire, clearly pictured himself as the President and won.

The question you should ask yourself is, "Do I have the ability to do something like that?" The answer is "yes," a definitive "yes"! This power of desire is one of the most amazing powers that we as life forms have. I heard a story once that a famous actor said he had the desire to make his dreams come true, but he was lucky that he met someone in an elevator who gave him a break. He simply did not realize that it was his desire that put him in the elevator at that moment. Fate has a way of putting you in the right place at the right time, if you have the desire to make something happen.

Another amazing success story is that of Tiger Woods. Tiger was only 2 years old when he made his first public appearance playing golf. He had appeared on a television talk show and played against the host Mike Douglas. He made a beautiful putt and beat Douglas in a putting contest live on television. It is truly an amazing thing to watch and I suggest you find a YouTube or other video of this feat to see it for yourself.

It is very clear that Tiger Woods wanted to be the greatest golfer in the world at a very young age. He didn't think that maybe it would be fun to play or maybe it would be a great weekend getaway, or a great time to play with clients; he clearly decided that he would be the greatest golfer and he is.

People like Tiger Woods spend countless hours working on perfecting the slightest detail on their game or effort. They not only practice a swing or a putt; they spend endless hours visualizing how that swing or putt should look.

How can you make your desire a reality? Here is the difficult part. The very first thing you need to do is to define what your desire truly is.

The question of the meaning of life is often referred to in philosophical conversations or even made the butt of jokes. However, it is as truly elusive as chasing the end of a rainbow for some of us. So many people go through life without a desire or purpose, which clearly leads to mediocrity.

Here is a great definition of *desire*. Desire is a destination, a goal, or something you will bet your life on.

I remember again back to my karate class days, when my instructor would tell us to close our eyes and visualize the condition we wanted to be in. What we would look like after being in great shape. He would often have us visualize ourselves in a full split or kicking a high mark on a target. The funny thing was that after about 2 years of class, I looked liked the person I had visualized and I was kicking right about where I had visualized as well.

The skeptic will argue that after 2 years of Karate you should be able to kick high and be in shape; this must be a poor example! Not quite. I want you to understand that after 2 years there were a few people in the class who never really changed much. They still could not kick high and probably never would, unless they truly desired it. However, the truly interesting part of this was the fact that there was a spot on the kicking bag that I wanted to hit with a round kick. This spot was as high as my nose and when I came to class for the first time all I could do was kick someone's ankles.

I stretched and stretched. I practiced my kick over and over. Sometimes I would even get close, but I could not hit it. I would even stay after class to practice and ask the instructor for special exercises that might help and then

I finally hit this spot. Funny thing though? I could never hit higher than that spot.

Now we have the double-edged sword of desire. If a desire is a goal to be obtained, does it then become a limiting factor as well? You see, as hard as I tried, I could never kick past this high spot on the kicking bag. As a matter of fact it wasn't long after hitting this spot that I completely dropped the class and never went back, even though I was only a month or two away from getting my black belt.

So what happened? I set a goal, a true desire: I wanted to kick that spot. That was it. I didn't realize that at the time it was the only thing that kept me going. As a matter of fact, I didn't go there every day and look at the spot and say "one day"; no, I went to class, learning balance and stretching my muscles, practicing stamina and kicking higher and higher each day, until *boom*! There it was, the perfect round-kick into that spot.

As I look back on other times of my life, I think about the desires I have had and find that I reached them and then drifted away from them. The most interesting goal was murmured over and over again as a child, as I blew out the candles on each birthday. I would make the same wish each year, "I wish I had a million dollars."

As time went on I got my wish. Yes, I had a net worth of over a million dollars just a few years ago. What I have learned is that first of all, a million dollars isn't really a lot of money, and second, that I should have wished for an annual income of a million dollars or at least something repeatable. Maybe I should have wished to keep the million dollars.

I just stated that a million dollars isn't all that much money, but if you have never had a million dollars or, like me, no longer have it, it truly becomes a large sum to accumulate. You and I, however, can accumulate that and more.

To do this, we need a plan to both make a million dollars (or whatever sum you desire) and still another plan to keep it. Someone once said that "if you make a million dollars and spend a million and one dollars, you are in debt." This is great advice and should be thought about when rereading the clichés and rules on money.

It all comes back to desire. You must first truly desire something to then acquire something. The question is, how much do you desire this? You must always understand that desires are not wishes. We will all wish for lots of money or wish for a new car or wish for a great love or wish to win the lottery. What I am talking about is a true passion, a burning desire of something you want. Is it money? And if it is, what is the exact amount that you desire? Not "I want a lot of it." If it is a million dollars, then make it that figure. My figure is five million in cash, stocks, and other liquid assets by the end of the year 2019. If your desire is a car, then what is the model of that car? You must be clear and concise and have that burning desire, and I assure you that you will achieve it.

I am sure that you can think of a time in your life that you truly wanted something and sometime later you had it. You should think about this moment and you may even find some other things you truly wanted that you later either have them or had.

I can honestly say that everything significant in my life was caused by the desire to get it. Your thoughts become your desires. You may see a car on the road that truly turns your head and think how much you want that car, and then a short time later you may actually have that car.

A few years back, an old acquaintance came back into my life and I invited him to my home for a drink and to meet my family. At the time I was living in a very affluent neighborhood and had a big home valued in today's dollars of about a million. As soon as we sat down he reminded me of something I had long forgotten. He said, "Larry, this is the street you told me you were going to live on." I had no idea what he was talking about, but I was amazed and asked him to elaborate. He explained that a few years ago we were driving down the intersecting road and I had pointed to this street and said, "I am going to live in one of these houses." Well, I was truly surprised, and I didn't remember that, but I am sure that it was true.

It is clear that desire works. It works for me and it will work for you. Prayer is also a method to obtain your desires. *"Very truly, I tell you, if you ask anything of the Father in my name, he will give it to you. Until now you have not asked for anything in my name. Ask and you will receive, so that your joy may be complete."* (John 16:23 - 24 NIV)

God will give you your desire if you ask Him for it clearly. If you pray for a thing, you will get it. Joel Osteen, a famous preacher, tells humorous stories of this. One that comes to mind is that of his mother who wanted a pool in the backyard. His mother asked his father time and time again for a swimming pool. He would always answer that it was too expensive and too much maintenance; he would not budge.

She was so determined to have this pool that she would often describe the backyard with the pool in it. On hot days, she would comment on how nice it would be to jump in and cool off. She even set up patio furniture to surround the would-be area of the pool. Now Joel's mom prayed for this pool and desired this pool so much that one day, out of the blue, while the Osteens were on a trip, they met a man who built pools. This man was so inspired by the speeches that the elder Osteen would preach that he wanted to return the favor by building them a pool at no cost. This, according to the Osteens, was completely unsolicited and took the family by surprise. Joel's mother got her pool and the kids took care of the maintenance. Her desire and prayers are clearly what led her to have her pool.1

For many people, praying for something when they are in dire straits or desperate does not work for them. Most preachers will tell you that you should pray and give thanks for the things you have. Another preacher once said not to worry about being petty in your prayers. This means that you can pray for the small things as well as the big things. Just recall, *"Ask and you will receive, so that your joy may be complete."* If you believe in God, then you know that God wants us to happy. Some of us feel that we should not waste a prayer on something trivial when millions suffer in the world. It is okay to ask God to put an end to the suffering and also ask God to help you find the money to replace your worn tires or anything else you need or need or desire.

When you pray or desire something, you must be filled with emotion and feeling in order to receive it. If you do not believe in God, then scientists have defined the "Law of Autosuggestion"2. This law states that "what you think you are, or what you think you want, is what you are or what you get." You have probably heard the statement, "If you think you can or you think you can't, you are probably right." This is a statement given in almost every motivational or sales training meeting. This statement is so true and real. I remember having a conversation with someone a few years back and saying, "Most millionaires go bankrupt twice." I know I heard this somewhere and maybe it is or isn't true, but it was a reality to me. I truly believed it. You may find it interesting that a year before writing this book, I was discharged from my second bankruptcy. I am now truly ready to be a real millionaire and I know I will be!

This book also came from desire. The success of this book will be up to my desire. It is my desire, thought, and prayer that it becomes a bestseller and gets featured in Oprah Winfrey's Book Club. I see myself sitting across from her on her stage discussing the book. She is smiling and reading the past passage and making comments on it. The audience is entranced.

Before I wrote this book, I had the desire to write a book on motivation. I truly had no idea what I would write, but I also knew that I could not type. I had gotten through most of my life without having to type, but I could hunt and peck very quickly. I knew, however, that if I wanted to keep up with my thoughts I needed to learn this skill that I had avoided until now. Before I even knew what I was going to write, I took a computer-based typing course. When I was about halfway through the course, ideas for the book started to come to me and I typed "Chapter One."

The difficult part comes in defining your true desires. The reason for most people not to pull themselves up from mediocrity is that they truly do not know what they desire. Imagine, if you would, that you were to venture into the Twilight Zone. There in front of you is the genie's lamp. Because you have seen this episode a few times, you rub the lamp, and out comes the genie. With a rumble in his voice he says, "You have three wishes!" Now you have to think. What would they be? Would you wish for a million dollars? Would you wish for world peace? Would you wish for love? Would you wish for diamonds? A big house, a new car? What would you wish for? Think about this for a moment. I often read self-help books and they usually have exercises for self-growth. I usually skip them over and never complete them, but I am asking you not to do this (unless of course you wrote one of the books with exercises I skipped over and want revenge). I am going to ask you to answer the following questions with intention and thought. When you answer these questions, do not answer them as "I wish" but answer them as "I will and can."

1) How much money do you want to make, annually?
2) What is your true dream house (where is it located, how big is it, even describe with as much detail as you can what it looks like)?
3) What is your dream job? Is it a title? Is it a way of life?
4) What activities make you happy?
5) What lifestyle do you think the "rich people" live?
6) What lifestyle do you want to live?
7) In the career path that you have currently chosen, can you reach these goals?
8) What do you see your retirement as being like? (Age of retirement, where you will be, how much money you will have, etc.)
9) Are you happy with your life and where you are now, and why or why not?
10) Which question was the most difficult for you and why?

If you truly answered these questions and gave it the thought it deserved, then you are already on the path to finding your desires.

I once met a man who, when he got to know you, would ask this simple question, "Where do you see yourself in 5 years?" He would not elaborate on the question even if you asked him for specifics. He just wanted the answer that came to the person when he asked. After I answered the question, I asked him why he asked. He went on to tell me that most people cannot answer that question in any detail. He found it amazing how unfocused most people are. I gave that some thought myself and now I often ask that question of others. I found that he was correct in his observation, and often mediocrity was truly the answer.

By the way, my answer was, "I see myself helping others with my books and seminars on self-help, motivation and sales. I see the changes in the lives I have touched, and I make a good living at it." It is interesting to note that I had this conversation at least two years before I learned to type.

In the next few chapters I will help you clarify and focus your desires. Get ready to learn much about yourself in them. For now, here is my next set of lottery numbers.

Remember, please read them out loud!

12 13 14 22 31 Powerball 11

Chapter 8

Fear vs. Desire

Have you ever truly thought about what you want out of this period on earth called "your life"? If you were to ask people on the street or the people you know that question, most would answer that they want happiness. This is an idealistic view of the question. In the rare circumstance of someone giving you a specific answer, you may actually find that person is either about to get what they want or is clearly on the path to getting what they want.

As I mentioned in the last chapter, throughout history so many have asked, "What is the meaning of life?" The real question each and every one of us should ask is, "What is the meaning of MY life?" When you take the time to think about this question, you truly begin on the path of self-discovery and possibly the path to great riches and happiness.

Many books have been written on these topics, such as *The Secret*, *The Purpose Driven Life*, and my personal favorite, *Think and Grow Rich*. Each one of these books reminds you that it is very important to fully understand your dreams and desires at all times in order to make them happen.

When I was younger, my mother insisted on telling me that I could be anything I wanted when I grew up. I am sure you have heard this and have even told your children the same thing. However, what does this statement really mean? Does it mean that if I wanted to be President that I could be? Well the answer is, of course, yes.

There are many excuses as to why people do not follow their dreams and desires. The biggest excuse comes under the label of "fear." Fear is one of the most damaging emotions that we as humans have. Fear comes from us wanting to be safe. It is clear that if a tornado is coming, we know we need to find shelter to protect ourselves. If there is a car speeding at us, fear helps us react to avoid the collision. Fear of injury or death is a very rational emotion, unless of course you are so fearful of death that it restricts your sense of adventure or enjoyment of normal life.

After the rational fears, what is left is different for all of us. The most common of fears that we as humans have is the fear of not being accepted or liked by our friends, peers, and even strangers. This fear holds us back from our desires. This fear causes us to live a so-called "normal" life. A "normal" life is usually a life without the necessary risks to meet the goals and desires we have.

Imagine that you have the great idea to quit your job and open an ice cream store. You do all of the research and have the capital. You have picked out a great location and you are all ready to start. You come home and tell your family, whether it is your wife or your parents, and say, "I quit my job today and tomorrow I am taking all we have saved to open an ice cream store!" I guarantee that no one, at that moment, would say, "That is wonderful, let's celebrate!" No, the answer would probably be more like, "Are you crazy?" "What if it fails?" "Ice cream, that is seasonal; what are you going to do in the winter?" And so on.

The fear of this response, the fear of losing your family or just the fear of the confrontation, may even be enough to keep you from giving this great idea a second thought. So we continue our "normal" life and get our paycheck from our hourly paying job and never realize the full potential inside ourselves.

Some others take a risk and go into sales. These people at least realize that their earnings are attached to their skill. Salespeople have a higher earning potential than people in most other professions. Salespeople usually earn commissions on what they sell and that is the majority of their income.

Salespeople, however, have the same fear of not being liked, or the fear of their friends feeling they are pushy. So what do they do? They often give into the fear and quit.

I once attended a sales seminar and the speaker expressed an interesting story. This story was to help eliminate the fear of selling services to a friend or relative. The speaker was trying to help salespeople overcome this fear. To help the audience, the speaker's story went something like this:

"If you heard a noise at 3 in the morning and looked out of your window to see that someone was breaking into your neighbor's garage, and this thief was stealing his brand new lawnmower, what would you do?" He went on to explain, "This is the lawnmower that your neighbor, Bob, had been telling you he was saving up for months to buy. He hadn't even used it more than twice. He paid a whopping $500 dollars for this amazing mower and he was proud to own it." The speaker continued, "Now with that information, would you roll over, go to bed and tell Bob about this in the morning, or would you call Bob right now?" He explained," You would be waking him up out of a deep sleep, disturbing his dog that will bark for an hour, possibly startling the other neighbors and of course the phone will wake his sleeping infant who won't go back to sleep for several hours.

"I believe you would still call Bob at 3 in the morning to tell him that someone was stealing the lawnmower," he explained. He then asked, "Would you have the same passion if you sold car insurance and knew that you could save Bob over $500 a year on his premium over the company that he was with? Remember, Bob is your friend," he continued. "Is this important to you? Would you think it may be important to Bob?"

Now the speaker went on about how you wouldn't have to call in at 3 am and wake everyone up. As a matter of fact, it could just be casual conversation the next time you went to Bob's house, for any reason at all. You could save Bob $500 and you would be building up your car insurance business.

I brought this up because most salespeople are so afraid to hear a friend like Bob say "no," or they are afraid of Bob not liking them because they dared to ask their friend for the appointment to explain how they could help save him money on his insurance.

These are examples of the fear of being disliked or the fear of criticism. Other irrational fears drive us to make poor decisions—or even worse, *no decision*. The fear of being alone when we are older or not finding our true love can be described as the fear of lost or forgotten love. The fear of "getting old" is another and is truly an irrational fear. I always laugh when someone says these two phrases: "You're not getting any younger!" or "You are getting older every day!" I find those two statements to be the most obvious statements ever. If you said those statements to a newborn baby they would mean the same thing!

The final fear is that of being poor. So many people are so afraid to be poor or unable to pay for the necessities that they just put their heads down and just work to pay the bills. This fear of being poor is what would rattle the minds of your family when you told them that you wanted to open an ice cream store with all of your savings. Most people wouldn't even have gone past the wishing stages into the research stages because of this fear. Most people, easily approaching 90%, don't push on beyond this fear.

Let's review these fears again:
1) Fear of death
2) Fear of being disliked or of criticism
3) Fear of being unloved
4) Fear of old age
5) Fear of being poor

On the contrary, here are the basic desires of all of us:
1) Desire to live a long or exciting life
2) Desire to be liked
3) Desire to be loved
4) Desire to be or feel young
5) Desire to be rich

If you look at these lists you will clearly see a sort of "tug of war" going on. You remember the game of "tug of war" from when you were a kid. In this game two teams would hold opposite ends of a rope. The rope would have a flag tied to the center, and your team would pull the rope while the other team at the other end would pull the rope in the opposite direction. The goal was to get the flag to your side and be declared the winner.

Fear and Desire is a simple game of "tug of war" and there is always a winner. It is either fear or desire. Sometimes you may decide not to play the game. This is the "fear" of playing the pre-game.

Take a moment to complete these two exercises to determine your fear and desire levels. On the number line below, circle the number that fits you the best. First you should look at your fears. 5 represents a great fear of something and 0 represents no fear. A good example of a fear of five would be this: Let's say you are deathly afraid of water. A 5 fear would be someone who would not even get into a 3-foot deep backyard pool or walk near the water on a beach because they feared drowning. A no fear or 0 on the scale would be someone who just jumps in whenever there is water; he or she probably has a boat and scuba dives often.

Now take a pen and circle the number that fits you best for your fear for each subject.

FEARS

←-5----4----3----2----1----0	Fear of death
←-5----4----3----2----1----0	Fear of criticism
←-5----4----3----2----1----0	Fear of being unloved or losing a love
←-5----4----3----2----1----0	Fear of old age
←-5----4----3----2----1----0	Fear of poverty

Next we will graph our desires. For the first one, "desire to live," you should think of it sort of like this: a number 5 is someone who may be a mountain climber or skydiver; a 1 may be someone who likes comfort living, like watching TV, reading, or other low-risk activities. Motorcycle riders probably fall in the 2-3 range, but this is your scale, so use your best judgment.

The desire to be liked would be someone who wants to mingle with everyone in a room. A five would probably be someone who likes to perform in front of a crowd. They may be an actor or a musician.

I think you get the idea. Now circle the number that fits your desire level.

DESIRES

Desire to truly live	0----1----2----3----4----5--→
Desire to be liked	0----1----2----3----4----5--→
Desire to be loved	0----1----2----3----4----5--→
Desire to feel young	0----1----2----3----4----5--→
Desire to be rich	0----1----2----3----4----5--→

If you were honest you should be starting to learn a little about yourself. Now you should take the exercise to the next level. On the graph below, average the numbers to see where on the number line you fall. For example, if you had a 3 in fear of death and a 2 in desire to live, you should circle 1 on the fear side as the average. Be honest and don't change your answers; there are no wrong answers or bad graphs.

Fear of...		Desire to...
Death	←-5--4--3--2--1--0--1--2--3--4--5-→	Live
Criticism	←-5--4--3--2--1--0--1--2--3--4--5-→	To be liked
Being unloved	←-5--4--3--2--1--0--1--2--3--4--5-→	To be loved
Growing old	←-5--4--3--2--1--0--1--2--3--4--5-→	Staying young
Poverty	←-5--4--3--2--1--0--1--2--3--4--5-→	To be rich

This is not a perfect science, but if you examine the graph, there are certain predictions of your current situation that can be assumed. First, the side that your circled number is on is the dominant side. What this means is that if you, for example, have circled a 3 on the left side of the graph for fear of poverty, then you are probably pretty broke right now. On the other hand, if you circled a 4 on the staying young side of the graph, you probably hear many people say that "you look so young" or "I can't believe that is your real age." You get the idea.

You will probably continue to find the same conclusion throughout the graph. If you are on the side of fear of criticism, you will find that you are criticized often or at least feel that way. If you are on the side of desire to live, you probably live an exciting life, or at least you are certainly not bored.

What does this all mean? It means that *fear will hold us back from our desire and the lack of desire will give us more fear."* Read that again and then I will explain: *fear will hold us back from our desire and the lack of desire will give us more fear.* Everyone has fear, but not everyone has desire. Some people have wishes but not true desires. Desires are the things you truly want out of life. Fears will also cause you to form the excuses of why you aren't getting your desires, and in the end the fear is what you end up with.

Take the middle-aged man who always wanted to be in shape. His fear is that he will get fat, unfit, unattractive, and unhealthy. His desire, however, is to be in good shape, attractive and healthy. His fear makes up excuses, like: "I hate getting up early to work out," " I hate lifting weights, they make me sweat," "I will have to take a shower in the middle of the work day," "I can't drink with my buddies because it is too many calories"; you get the picture. So what happens when his fear is dominating his desire? He becomes fatter and more out of shape every day. This is exactly what he fears! Instead he should increase his desire to be in shape, and then he surely would get into the shape he wants.

It is the same with money. If your dominating side is the fear of poverty, then you will make up excuses not to be rich. Some of these may sound familiar: " How can I put 10% of my money away when I can't even pay my bills?", "I can't call and negotiate a lower payment on my accounts, they are a big company and they will say no," "I can't invest money in the stock market, I always lose it" (you lose it because the fear of losing it is dominating!), and of course, "If I could only win the lottery then all my problems would go away!" If your fear of poverty is dominating, then this may have sounded pretty familiar.

It is important to understand that all people, rich and poor, have fears. The rich people simply have a stronger desire to be rich, and the poor people have more fear of poverty.

As I write this book, I have the fear of criticism. I worry if people will like the book. What if I can't get it published? I worry about the reviews, the critics, and I hope you are enjoying it. However, my fear level is low and my desire level is off the charts. I will finish this book, if the world likes or not. Then I will have fulfilled my desire to write it. That is the power of desire!

In the past chapter, I asked you to answer the listed questions. If you did this, when you came to the last question, was it the hardest to answer? For those who answered that question 10 was the hardest, you avoided the answer. The reason it was hard was because you had to overcome the fear of self-criticism. Have you heard the expression "I am my own worst critic"? YOU are often the hardest to please and YOU will make your life miserable if you can't accept YOU for who you are. Before you can get over the fear of criticism from others, you must get over the fear of your own criticism.

Now that we know that a stronger desire can counteract fears, and less fear can encourage desire, how shall we proceed? First realize that the fear will disappear if you are moving toward your desires. Think about this: do people who have a million dollars or more, in a savings account, fear poverty? Probably not. So with that knowledge it is easy to understand that if we reach our desires, or at least start on the path to our desires, then our fear will diminish and our desire will increase, causing the fear to diminish further, causing the desire to increase further, and so on. Imagine re-graphing the example above and all of your numbers are 4 or 5 on the desire side. Can you imagine what your life would be like then? I would imagine that you would be very happy with your progress indeed.

The next chapter will help you overcome these fears and get excited about your desires. Don't be afraid of what you will find out about yourself; instead, have the desire to learn and conquer the fear of your self-knowledge.

Now for my next set of lottery numbers.

Remember to please read them out loud!

12 14 25 31 41   Powerball 11

Chapter 9

Overcome the Fear and Reach For the Stars!

If you are a parent or have been around a child, you certainly remember them asking the same question over and over again. The question is "why?" They would say, "Why, Mommy?", "Why, Daddy?", "Why is this…", "Why is that…", "Why, why, why?" Believe it or not, this question is truly the answer to your desires and reaching your dreams. Let me explain simply by saying that you must know *why* you have a desire.

If you want to be rich you must know *why*. If you want to live an exciting life, you must know *why*. If you want to spend your life with a loved one, then you must know *why*. This is probably the hardest thing for most of us to understand. "Why," you ask? Because we simply don't give it any thought. We go through life oblivious to what is going on around us. We simply go to work to make money to buy food and provide shelter for ourselves and our families. The "why?" for food and shelter is built into our programming. The basic necessities for humans to live are food and shelter. For the most part, we as humans provide these instinctually. Everything else we need or want is not instinct but what we need to actually think about in order to accomplish.

In the example of the number line of our fears and desires (in the last chapter), you may have realized that your thoughts may be your enemy, preventing you from accomplishing your desires. If you are thinking about the fear of poverty, then you probably scored 3 or higher on the scale toward poverty. As we already concluded, you are probably pretty broke right now. Think about this: is it the fact that you are broke making you fear poverty, or is it your fear of poverty that makes you broke? I tell you for sure that it is your thoughts and fears of poverty that are making you broke.

I remember a great experiment that a motivational trainer once demonstrated. He told a group of us (and you should try this on yourself or a friend) to close our eyes. While our eyes were closed he asked us to think of the color blue. He described blue in different ways. He talked about blue skies and blue water. He helped us draw mental pictures with blue in them. All about the color blue. He went on and on. He then asked us to open our eyes slowly. As we did he said to look around and see all of the blue in the room. To my amazement, the blue in the room stood out over every other color. Blue in pictures on the wall stood out, blue on the notebooks of some of the attendees stood out. Even the blue eyes of some of the participants in the class stood out. I would bet that while you are reading this, you have noticed blue in the room you are in.

So what does this all mean? It simply means that what you think about is what you will have. Yes, this is true! If you think about being broke, you are! If you think about being fat, you are! If you think about being alone, then again, you are. You must start to think on the other side of the number line. You must think about your desires.

The first step in thinking about your desires is to identify them. What do you really want out of life? In chapter 7, I asked you to take the time to answer 9 questions. The first was, "How much money do you want to make, annualized?" I hope you took the time to think about the question and I hope you answered it. How would it feel to make that much money? Now add another 25%. How would it feel to make that much money? Add 50%. That's right: if you said $100,000 a year, add another $50,000 for a total of $150,000.

Does adding the 20% or 50% make you feel uncomfortable? How much money makes you feel uncomfortable? Are you uncomfortable making $200,000 a year, $500,000 a year, or $1,000,000 a year? Some of you answered the question, "How much do you want to make?", with an answer that is only about 10% or 20% more than you are making now. This answer may be the root of the reason why you are not rich or why you are not reaching your dreams. This is the fear of money!

There is actually a name for the fear of money. It is called Chrematophobia. This fear brings on these symptoms, in varying degrees of severity: breathlessness, light-headedness, excessive sweating, queasiness, dry mouth, shuddering, and heart palpitations. Can you believe it? A fear of money! This fear can actually cause people to be afraid of making more money.

As we discussed, fears bring excuses. The excuses you will probably hear from those afraid of making money will sound something like this: "Rich people are mean," "I won't have time to spend with my family because I will be working too hard to earn," "Money isn't everything, you know," "I will have to pay more taxes," "Money brings new problems," and so on. Did some of these sound familiar?

Let's take a step back for a moment and discuss your "why." Make a list of what is important to you in order of importance. Really think about this before you start writing. Put a minimum of 5 things in this list with number 1 being the most important. It is okay to shuffle the list if you find that something you just added at number 4 should be a number 2. If 5 items aren't enough, then keep going. Use the blanks below and really give it some thought.

List of what is important to me:

1) —————————————————————— *Number 1 importance!*

2) ——————————————————————

3) ——————————————————————

4) ——————————————————————

5) ——————————————————————

6) ——————————————————————

7) ——————————————————————

Now take a moment to review this list. Because each list is personal it is hard to predict your personal situation, but here are some common answers: "I want to spend more time with my children, spouse or family," "I want to travel," I want to relax and smell the roses," "I want to retire young," "I want a big house with land," "I want to move to another coast," "I want to help people," "I want to volunteer or participate in a charity," "I want to spend more time in church and study my religion," "I want to take care of a sick or dying relative," and many others.

You may have had one of these or a variation of one these in your list. Now take a moment to think about what is stopping you. The two most common answers are time and money. The first thing we will discuss is money.

How much money do you need to do the number one thing on your list? How much do you need to do number 2, number 3 and so on? Now you have a defined desire for money and the amount you need. (We will talk about how to get it in the following chapter, but at least you know or have a good idea how much you need.) I am sure that you noticed several of the things on the list do not need money at all. Just add up the other items that will cost money and fill in the sentence with the amount you feel you will need to accomplish your written desires.

I NEED EXACTLY $_____
TO ACCOMPLISH MY DESIRES.

The next topic is time. Did you know that both rich and poor people have the same amount of hours in a work week? There are exactly 168 hours in a 7-day week. How strange is it that people who do not realize their desires often use the same excuse to not reach them: "I don't have the time!"

Time is something you choose to use effectively or not. It does not mean that you have work 14 hours a day, 7 days a week. It means that you need to budget your time or have set hours during which you are willing to work on your desires. Just like your money, you must put aside a percentage of time or piece of each day to better yourself and to work on your desires.

At the time of writing this book, I am working a full-time 8-hour-a-day job, and it takes me a minimum of 1 ½ hours to travel to that job and a minimum of 1 ½ hours to travel home. That means that I have 11 hours a day dedicated to my full-time job. You would never hear me say that I don't have the time to work on my book, or frankly you would not be reading it right now.

If you budget an hour a day to work on yourself and your desires, you will find that you have found time that you didn't know existed. I often hear people say, "How do you find the time?" Well, on my desire number line, the time to better myself is very high.

Let's create a fantasy. All of a sudden you have 26 hours a day instead of 24 hours a day. If you could add these two hours of time into each day, what would you do with that time? Break it into pieces to make it easier, 15-minute intervals for example, and it may look like this:

1) 15 minutes   Read self-help books
2) 15 minutes   Exercise
3) 15 minutes   Meditation and/or prayer
4) 15 minutes   Research my desired career and start to design and work on that plan to make it happen.
5) 15 minutes   Research and order the next book or class I have an interest in.
6) 15 minutes   Have a quality conversation with my loved ones before they leave for work in the morning.
7) 30 minutes   Study work or homework for any classes I am now taking.

Now take a moment and design your own two hours. I know, I know: you don't have the time to design your 2 hours, or what's the point since you won't find two hours anyway? **Just do it!**

Time interval	What I would do with it
15 minutes	
15 minutes	
15 minutes	
15 minutes	
15 minutes	
15 minutes	
15 minutes	
15 minutes	

Now, if you have designed your own 2 hours, then you are at the beginning of your proper time control. If these desires are high enough, I bet you will wake up early to start your day and work on them. I awake each day at 5 am and go for a 45-minute walk. About two years ago, I herniated 2 disks in my back. It was so bad that I laid in bed and cried. I ended up having 2 epidurals to relieve the pain. The damage to my nerves was so severe that I had to walk with a cane because my left leg was weak and numb.

Each day I would wake up and dread getting out of bed because I would be afraid to fall. One day I decided that I could either walk in pain and with the help of a cane, or I could strengthen my muscles and nerves by walking daily. That day was the beginning of many steps to healing my back and leg; on that day I got up at 5 am and I walked. I walked for about 2 1/2 miles. When I got home that day I hurt and I was miserable. But the funny thing is that after 2 more days of walking I felt better and the cane was put aside.

My desire to walk overcame my fear of not walking *ever again*. My desire to be able to continue to use my legs also motivates me to walk each day and get up at 5 am. I have missed very few days of my walks and I have noticed that if I don't walk for two days in a row, the third day is difficult. In other words, I find the time to walk because it is my desire not to walk with a cane or need a wheelchair in the future.

Let's take this imaginary time of 2 hours and make it a reality. I already told you that I need 11 hours a day just for my primary work. So don't tell me it is impossible to find time. I assure you that if you watch a little less TV or spend a little less time on useless Internet sites you will find these two hours. Wake up an hour earlier to find one of the hours and the other hour will be easy to find by changing your priorities and your use of time.

Now that you know you can find the time, all you need is your desire to do it. Use the fear/desire number line to help you overcome your fears. A set of *fear/desire number lines*, as discussed in chapter 7, is a tool that you can use for anything that you think about. It is so simple to use and it can be used for both general desires and very specific desires. For example, if you want to lose weight, a fear/desire number line set might look this:

←-5----4----3----2----1----0   My fear of a heart attack

←-5----4----3----2----1----0   My fear my clothes may be too small

←-5----4----3----2----1----0   My fear I will not be attractive

←-5----4----3----2----1----0   My fear of loosing the attention I get
                                 because I am overweight

I desire to have a healthy heart   0----1----2----3----4----5--→

I desire to have my clothes look   0----1----2----3----4----5--→
good on me

I desire to be attractive   0----1----2----3----4----5--→

I desire to get attention for   0----1----2----3----4----5--→
being in good shape

Heart attack   ←-5--4--3--2--1--0--1--2--3--4--5-→ Healthy heart

Look bad   Look good
in clothes   ←-5--4--3--2--1--0--1--2--3--4--5-→   in clothes

Be unattractive ←-5--4--3--2--1--0--1--2--3--4--5-→   Be attractive

Not be liked   ←-5--4--3--2--1--0--1--2--3--4--5-→   Be liked

As you may recall from the previous example in the past chapter, if you are on the left side you are probably experiencing your fear. If you scored a 3 toward heart attack, you are probably in danger already. If you are afraid your clothes won't fit… well, you guessed it, I bet they are tight.

If you decide to overcome your fears and your desire is strong, you can use the number line to make good decisions during the day. For example, the girls at work are going out to lunch. They decide to go a diner. You are the last to order and all three of them ordered a hamburger. Here is the process…

←-5----4----3----2----1----0   My fear of gaining weight

←-5----4----3----2----1----0   My fear that if I order a salad everyone will laugh at me

←-5----4----3----2----1----0   My fear that I will want the hamburger that they ordered

I desire to lose weight   0----1----2----3----4----5--→

I desire not to be laughed at because I am fat   0----1----2----3----4----5--→

I desire to eat what makes me healthy   0----1----2----3----4----5--→

Fear to gain weight ←-5--4--3--2--1--0--1--2--3--4--5-→ Desire to lose weight

Fear of ridicule ←-5--4--3--2--1--0--1--2--3--4--5-→ Desire for compliments

Fear of missing out ←-5--4--3--2--1--0--1--2--3--4--5-→ Desire to be healthy

Remember also that the fear side brings out the excuses, and remember that the desire side brings on the motivation. If you find yourself making excuses, then stop and think of the number line. Is fear winning? Can you increase your desire to motivate yourself? Think of the desire, not the fear, and you will get what you want out of life. Oh, and order the salad.

Finally, I want you to set your desires high. This is very important. Did you ever hear the expression "reach for the stars and you may get the moon"? I want you to go back to your needed amount of money and increase it by 30%. Just turn back to that page and put a line through your previous number. Write next to it the number increased by 30%. I want you to reach for the stars! Forget the moon and go for it! If you needed a million dollars to reach your desires, then now your goal is a million three hundred thousand. If you got it, would you be upset? I think not. Remember my karate round kick, the one where I reached my goal and could never kick higher? Well, my goal was too low. Don't make the same mistake.

Before you go to the next chapter, take out a piece of paper and draw fear/desire number line set for the top 3 desires that come to your mind. It may be about money, weight loss, a job offer, deciding to get married or stay married, or anything that comes to mind. After you complete the number lines, write down the excuses that your fears are creating and then write down the motivations that will make your desires come true.

Remember again that if you were honest, then the side of the number line that you are currently on is the path you are headed down. If you are on the fear side, then you are probably making excuses as to why you can't accomplish the opposing desire. If the desire side is dominating, then you are probably thinking of the ways to make this goal happen and it has already started to happen. Your goal should be to continue to make the desire stronger. Don't be discouraged if you are on the left side, the fear side; just take a deep breath and know that you can counter this fear with your desire, thus changing the path you are on.

I think that this quote from Barack Obama says it all: "If you're walking down the right path and you're willing to keep walking, eventually you'll make progress." 1

Now for my next set of lottery numbers.

Remember to please read them out loud!

18 23 30 34 49   Powerball 11

Chapter 10

Your $25,000,000

In chapter 6 I had the opportunity to describe, in detail, what I would do if I won $25,000,000 in the lottery. You probably moaned and groaned all through reading it. You made internal statements like, "I wouldn't do that, I would do this," or, "That part is a good idea," or maybe you thought I was stingy when it came to the money I would give away, or maybe you just thought, "Yeah right, we will see if he does that if and when he wins!" Well, I assure you that these are my plans and I will execute them with precision when it happens.

Now it is your turn…. You turn on the TV and watch the lucky numbers get drawn. One by one they match your numbers on your ticket. Then the Powerball gets picked and HOORAY! You are the holder of the winning ticket! You just won $25,000,000 after taxes in cash. What are you going to do? Are you going to squander it? Are you going to hate yourself? Are you going to be living in a trailer in a few years or think it is a curse?

Well, here is some help. Fill in some of these questions and, if you are so inclined, you may even want to add some others.

Your $25,000,000

> *I suggest you use a separate piece of paper for this exercise, or, even better, a word processing program, so that you can add to or change your answers as time goes by.*

- How much will you put away for safe keeping? This would go into your untouchable account.
  $_____
- Will you create an annuity account that will pay you a set figure for a set time? If yes, how much income do you want?

(Using a conservative 4% return, calculate how much you will need to put in an annuity. Here is a hint: for a 40-year annuity, you will need $1,000,000 for an annual sum of $48,500.)
$_____

- Describe the house you would want to live in. Where do you want to live? _____

  _____

  _____

  _____

- Describe the state, city and town. Do you want land or to live in a high rise? (Is it near the water, mountains, a specific place? Make your description as detailed and accurate as possible. Use a separate paper to really detail it all.) _____

  _____

  _____

  _____

- How much are you going to need for this home?
  $_____

- Are you going to buy a second or third home?

- Describe these in detail as well. How much will you need for this/these home(s)?
  $_____

- What type of car will you drive? Will there be more than one?

  _____

  _____

  _____

- Describe the make and model of these cars. How much will you allocate for the cars?
  _____

- Gifts for others. If you are allocating a lump sum gift for family members to be split among them, put in the lump sum and how much for each person. List their names and the amounts.

  _____

  _____

  _____

- Will you put any restrictions on how it will be spent? If yes, what are the restrictions and why? Enter the lump sum needed for this. $_____

- Will you make a special party or celebration for friends? Describe that in detail.

  _____
  _____
  _____

- How much will the party cost?
  $_____

- Now the fun stuff: special jewelry such as a watch or necklace, a boat, an antique car; list them all and put a price next to them.

  _____
  _____
  _____
  _____

- How much will you allocate to charities, or to your church or other house of worship? Detail the total amount and then the amount to each, and also add to the list why you want to help that charity. Is it because you know someone who is suffering from a disease and wish to help? Is it to feed the poor? Is it to save animals, or maybe to build a wing in your church? _____

  _____
  _____
  _____

- Detail why you want to help these specific charities. _____

  _____
  _____
  _____

- If you are buying a home or houses, how much are you going to use for furniture? And what will you buy?
  $_____

  _____
  _____
  _____

- List any trips you want to take in detail. What are the destinations? How long are you going to go there for? Why do you want to go there?

  _____

  _____

  _____

- How much do you need for these trips?

  $_____

The above was to get you started making a list of things you would spend this money on. Make sure you put the amount of the cost next to the item and subtract that from the original $25,000,000. Don't go broke with $25,000,000!

Some other ideas for your list may include putting someone in business or buying your own business, helping out friends, expanding a business, buying collectables such as art or cars, or others. How about friends or relatives that may need medical attention or equipment that they could not get without your help? Keep thinking and adding to your list, but make sure that you keep writing how much you would allocate to each, and make sure you do not spend more than the $25,000,000.

Take your time with this list and make it accurate. Remember that you probably won't win the lottery again, so when the $25,000,000 is used up, it cannot be replaced.

Now review your list. Ask yourself some important questions. The first is, did you remember to use the clichés (rules) of money? Did you make sure that you didn't spend it all? Do you have sufficient funds put aside for emergencies or other events? Did you plan to have a sufficient income?

Can you afford to do everything on your list? More importantly, will doing all of these things make you happy, or will they make you crazy trying to make them all happen? Remember that you can adjust this list at any time to meet your needs and desires, but you will never have another $25,000,000 after it is gone.

Take your list and dig even deeper now. Start to look for the things on your list. For example, if you wanted a house on the beach in Florida, go to real estate websites and look for houses in the price range that match your list. Go to the websites of the car manufacturers for the cars that you want to buy. For example, if it is a Mercedes, go to the page on the website that takes you to the "build your car" option and build it online. Select your car, then select the interior and exterior colors and all of the options that you want.

For charities, find out more about that charity and the people involved. The Internet makes such easy work of this, but don't get lazy. Look deep into the information and decide which organization will help the cause you are interested in to the best of your desires.

Remember: you are the holder of the responsibility of $25,000,000. This responsibility has great power, so don't blow it!

Now close your eyes and think about all of the things on your list. Picture the colors of the items, the satisfaction you got from donating to a charity. Picture yourself in your new home on your new furniture, surrounded by the things you bought. Picture yourself in your new car, driving to the golf course, or the beach, or anywhere you like. Picture yourself on the trip or trips you have planned.

Picture it all and enjoy this moment of thinking about it. Dream tonight about it and discuss it with your significant other. Really enjoy the thought.

But first, my next set of lottery numbers.

Remember to read them out loud, please!

14 22 24 32 41 Powerball 11

Chapter 11

What We Think About...

How did it feel to think about the trips, the cars, and the house you would own if you won the $25,000,000? Did you see yourself on a sunny day, as I did, driving your version of the Cadillac XLR- V convertible, pulling in to the four-car garage of the Florida home? Or maybe it was a feeling of satisfaction as you funded your church or synagogue's expansion. Maybe you imagined being on the trip of your dreams with the person you love, soaking in the sun and just relaxing.

Now answer this: "What have you been thinking about all day?" I bet it was your job, or the traffic you were waiting in to get there. Maybe you thought about your boss whom you and everyone else at work dislike. Maybe it was the money problems you are having, or maybe it was a fight with your spouse. Now ask yourself, "How often are these the *primary thoughts* in your head?" It is time for you to realize that your thoughts guide your life.

Once we know our thoughts guide our lives, we then learn how we can change our thoughts and thereby change our lives. We first must focus our thoughts on what we want to accomplish, thereby accomplishing what we think about. If you don't believe me, try this experiment: think of something awful, maybe a news story you heard today or a friend's hard luck story. While you think of this, make a deep frown with your mouth. Now make it even deeper. Did you notice your mood changed?

Now try this: think of something happy. Maybe it is a recent accomplishment or something that your child did that you are proud of. Now smile as giddily as you can. Show your teeth and smile really widely. Did you notice how your mood shifted again? If you are like most people, you noticed right away that you felt better when you smiled and thought your happy thought. When you frowned, you felt kind of down and miserable.

With this experiment in mind, you must change your thoughts to happy and productive thoughts. You must do this whenever you are feeling anything but happy and productive. Something I have observed is that it is easier to feel miserable and continue to feel miserable than to take your thoughts into your own control and change them. I assure you that with practice and a little work you can think yourself happier and more productive.

Now is the time to look at your $25,000,000 spending spree from the last chapter. I would imagine that you were pretty aggressive with your thoughts on how to spend it. In a prior chapter, I asked you to think about some of the things and the career you want. Now take your list of the things you would buy with your $25,000,000. Think about the career you want and imagine that you had this career. Imagine that it funded all the things you wanted when you listed the things you chose to buy with your winnings.

Think about these things and how your life would be when you were there. Think about the home you would live in, the car you would drive, the food you would eat. Think about the friends you would have and the vacations you would take. Think about it as though you are living it right now.

It is time for your notepad again. Write down what your life is like 10 years from now. Write it in present tense. Write it as detailed as you like, but remember to write everything you feel is important. This is what mine looks like:

My Future in 10 years

- I have a house with the beach or a dock in the back
- I have a 42-foot sailboat
- I have a convertible for fun, a Cadillac XLR V
- I have organized charities and I help people
- I am teaching and training others
- I have written a best-selling book on motivation, one on sales, and others
- I have people who respect me and I respect them
- I have mastered the skills of keeping and understanding money
- I have $12 million in several accounts that I treat with respect
- I can live a life without working, but I continue to work because it is rewarding
- I am married to Carol, the woman I love, and we share a great life together

Now post this list on a refrigerator or a door, or somewhere you can see it often. Read it out loud often, preferably every day. When you read this list, you must believe with all your heart and soul that you currently have these things. You must read it with the emotion it deserves. You must picture yourself, there in the future, with the items on your list.

If you truly believe in something and put it out in the universe and let God hear it, you will receive it. If you believe in God, then you believe the Bible phrase *"ask, and you will receive, that your joy may be made full"* (John 16:27 NAS). If you believe in a higher power, in the universe and the great power bestowed on us, then you will believe that you can make this power transform your desires into realty. Faith is all it takes. It may be faith in God or faith in a higher power you cannot understand, but you must have faith. With faith all will be granted!

You may be starting to understand why I have asked you to read my lottery numbers out loud. This is to put those numbers out there in front of the higher power. The repetition of all the people reading this book and reading those numbers will cause the numbers to be picked. The more people who read them out loud, the more power will be created to manifest these numbers to be drawn.

A great lottery example of this was on Wednesday, September 11, 2002. This was the one-year anniversary of the worst disaster in United States history. An interesting phenomenon happened that day in the lottery. Because the tragedy was so fresh in so many minds, several people played the New York pick 3 lottery. The amazing part was that they all won, and yes, you guessed it: the numbers, in order, were 9-1-1. If you don't believe me, look it up! It is true!

Take a moment and look at this Fear/Desire graph of what I am asking you to do. Make the marks honestly as described in the previous chapters.

←-5----4----3----2----1----0	My fear that my spouse or children will think I am silly
←-5----4----3----2----1----0	My fear that it won't really happen
←-5----4----3----2----1----0	My fear that it will happen and I will have to believe

I desire to have my wishes	0----1----2----3----4----5--→
I desire to have my dream occupation	0----1----2----3----4----5--→
I desire faith	0----1----2----3----4----5--→

Remember, subtract the fear number from the desire number and plot it on a total graph.

Fear of being silly	←-5--4--3--2--1--0--1--2--3--4--5-→	Desire to have my wishes
Fear it won't happen	←-5--4--3--2--1--0--1--2--3--4--5-→	Desire to be what I want
Fear of a higher power	←-5--4--3--2--1--0--1--2--3--4--5-→	Desire for help from faith

If your number line is to the left, then you are probably making excuses right now. Excuses that probably sound like this: "This is bull," "This won't work", "Higher power, yeah right," "This won't happen". Stop saying those things, RIGHT NOW!

Remember the smile exercise? Now is the time to try it again. Think of one or several things on your list and smile widely; show your teeth and make it as giddy as you can. Now go back and change your number line to be on the right side. Give yourself the courage to have the desire to make it work.

If your desire was already strong and you thought thoughts like "wow, this is great," "that felt so great to write it and read it," "I can't wait to have all of this," then you are truly ready to start receiving the blessings that will be bestowed on you by your belief. To continue this belief you can try using affirmations.

Affirmations are another great way of getting your mindset in the right direction. I first heard of affirmations a few years ago. Affirmations are the things you say to yourself to make you feel better or stronger. You probably didn't realize that you often used affirmations in your past without knowing it. Picture a young child in gym class staring at the rope he is about to climb. He starts murmuring, "I can do this, I can do this, I can do this," and he does! That is an example of a simple affirmation.

Some of the affirmations I remember going through in sales training classes sounded like this: "I am a superstar salesperson!" "I can sell ice to an Eskimo!" "I am super confident and no one can resist my sales charm."

I am getting tingly just writing them.

Now you need to create affirmations based on what you truly want out of life. I have listed some to get you started. Feel free to use any of the ones you like, but try to add some of your own. Remember they are desires, so make them explicit.

My Affirmations:
- I am an awesome writer and I will have a best-selling book
- I am great with finances
- I am a money-making machine
- I am a great motivator and will help thousands of people
- I have learned so much from my previous relationships that I will make the perfect husband.
- I will have the house, car, and boat of my dreams
- I will have a great day today, because how I perceive the world is in my control!

Now take out your notepad and write down your affirmations. Put them in a safe place and read them daily before you start your day.

I had a personal business coach also give me a great idea for this. She had another coach friend of hers who would call her each day at 6 am. He would read his affirmations to her and she would read her affirmations to him. I do have to admit that she was one of the most motivated people I had ever met. I still have not started doing that, but I just may start soon. Maybe you should also.

Never forget that you have control over your thoughts and your actions. These thoughts and actions will create your world as you know it. Take the negative out of your thoughts, accentuate the positive thoughts, and watch your life change in ways you never knew it could.

Now use what you have learned to make me (us) the next $25,000,000 lottery winner.

Read my next set of Powerball numbers very loudly.

2 6 12 14 33 Powerball 11

Chapter 12

Income

Income, as defined by the IRS, is: *Wages, salaries, tips, etc, Taxable interest, Dividends, Taxable refunds, credits or offsets of State and local income taxes, Alimony, Business income, Capital gain, Other gains, Taxable amount of individual retirement account (IRA) distributions, Taxable amount of pension and annuity payments, Rental real estate, royalties, partnerships, S corporations, trusts, etc., Farm income, Unemployment compensation payments, Taxable amount of Social Security benefits, Other income. (Includes: prizes and awards; gambling, lottery or raffle winnings; jury duty fees; Alaska Permanent fund dividends; reimbursements for amounts deducted in previous years; income from the rental of property if not in the business of renting such property; and income from an activity not engaged in for profit).* 1

Leave it to the IRS to really complicate things!

How many of the above incomes do you have? Most of us have only one and some of us have none! Because the IRS definition is so complicated, I have broken income into more understandable categories. They are as follows:

Income types
      1.   Wages, Salary
      2.   Passive Income
      3.   Residual Income
      4.   Investment Income
      5.   Growth Income

The first, wages or salary, is the income type most people are familiar with. It is the income derived from going to your job and receiving a paycheck. These wages may be an hourly rate or a fixed salary, or maybe commissions or bonuses. If you have a job that pays you that way, this usually means you are an employee of a company. That means that you are dependent on someone else to give you money for simply showing up for your job.

I wrote "simply showing up" because it is true. According to most of the labor laws in this country, if you showed up at your place of employment, you must be paid the wages that were agreed to when you were hired. This means that whether you are working harder than anyone else or "hardly working," you will still get a "day's pay." Of course, if you make a habit of not working hard you will probably be fired and replaced.

So what does this mean? Simply, it is the path to mediocrity. If I am the most productive employee in the widget-making shop and I make the same amount of money as the least productive employee, how long do you think I am going to continue at that pace? For most people, they won't stay highly productive very long. The least productive employee may be smart enough to realize that he needs to ramp it up a little bit to preserve his job. He then does the least it takes to keep the boss off his back. The company ends up with production at a low average, and it goes on and on.

I know what you are thinking: if the most productive employee keeps his production up, won't he get a promotion? Not at all! Think about this: if you owned a widget-making shop and you had one employee who produced 50% more widgets than the average employee, why would you take him away from that position? It would take 2 or 3 people to replace his productivity. That would cost 2 or 3 times the salary of the one promoted employee.

Did you ever wonder why the low to medium producers (or as most of you are thinking, the idiots) are the ones who get promoted? Now you understand why. Make a low producer a manager and the high producer will continue to make the most widgets. The new manager wasn't producing much in his old capacity, so this may just be an improvement. If not, there are several other low to medium producers out there to promote over the high producer. It is all about production and profit!

Wages and salaries are the income that we have been taught about our whole lives. Do well in school, go to college, and get a good job! Isn't that what our parents tell us? Well, how is that working for you? An even better question is, how did it work for your parents? I would bet that if your parents are really rich, they got there using the other types of income, not just their salaries.

The biggest problem with wage income is that it is always a temporary type of income. Wage income always has an end date. Sometimes the end date is by our choice and other times the end date is unexpected. If you retire, your wage-earning power is usually zero, or at best a smaller percentage of the original wage income. If you are suddenly let go from a job due to extraneous circumstances, such as lay-offs, plant closings, or being fired, you will lose your wages income. It is true that you can find another job, but you can't always depend on finding a job with the same wages, or even finding one quickly.

I want to briefly mention Unemployment Insurance. Unemployment Insurance from your local government should never be considered "income"; it is simply "insurance." Insurance is designed to help you with a financial loss and that is it. If you lost your job and you are collecting this *insurance*, then you must get back to work as soon as possible to start collecting wage income.

Never make the mistake of thinking you can collect more from your insurance than a job will pay you. First of all the insurance is more temporary than a wage income, as it is a time-limited benefit. It often ends after 26 weeks. If you are collecting more than you can earn from a job offer, it would be an unwise decision to stay unemployed and collect the insurance.

Keep in mind that for each month you are collecting unemployment insurance, your worth to a new employer diminishes. Also the motivation to work will start to diminish and you may actually end up depressed or feeling worthless. Can you imagine going to a job interview feeling worthless or depressed? The prospective employer will probably pick someone else. They may also feel that you have been out of work too long, and then they have the power to negotiate a lower starting pay than for someone who appears less desperate than you. Your earning power will clearly decrease for each month you are out of work. This will cause you to lose much more than you gained on your so-called "vacation" paid by the government.

Of course if you are really trying to get re-employed and still haven't found something, then consider yourself fortunate to be collecting the unemployment insurance. Only you can decide if you are "milking the system" or are truly in need.

Back to wages. The biggest benefit to wages income is the fact that you get paid quickly for your efforts. If you start a job on Monday, you can be pretty sure that you will receive your agreed pay in a pay cycle that is steady and fairly immediate. Usually pay cycles are weekly or bi-weekly, and you know the pay dates and the amount you will receive for each payment.

As for the other types of income on the list, they all require effort or time that will not be immediately rewarded. For example, as I write this book, I am not being paid for my time. In fact, I won't be paid until long after I have typed the final word. I also have no idea how much I will make in future sales of the book.

Other types of income are more permanent sources of income. They are unlike the temporary nature of wages income. Study each description and try to think of other examples besides those given in this book of these types of incomes.

Passive income is the next on the list. This is a great source of income because you do little to earn it. Imagine going on vacation for 5 weeks and telling your boss at your salary job, "Just forward my paycheck to the Fiji islands for the next 5 weeks. I am going to be there for a while." Yeah right! But imagine that you have a steady stream of income that pays you no matter where you are or what you do. This is passive income!

Passive income is derived from something you did a while back that creates its own income. A good example is rental income (assuming you have positive cash flow). Rental income is income from real estate that pays you month after month with some degree of certainty. If you go away to the Fiji islands for 5 weeks, your tenants still have to pay rent.

Other forms of passive income may include artistic works like a musician who produces an album. Each time the album is sold, the band gets a royalty check. You could also write a book and get passive income in the form of royalties. If you bought this book then I made about $3 in passive income. If you borrowed it, go buy your own copy, I want my passive income!

Passive income also comes in another way. Do you remember the example above of the widget makers? Let's say the widget makers are making widgets and the sales staff is selling the widgets at a profit. Because of this, the owner of the widget-making company is making residual income from each productive employee in the factory. Think about it, if the owner of the company goes on vacation for 5 weeks and his factory is still running and his salespeople are still selling, does the owner lose any income? I should say not. Therefore the power of passive income creates freedom.

Next on the list is residual income. Residual income is another form of passive income that has the same power but takes even less work to earn. This is income that you receive again and again from the sale of a single product sold only once to the consumer. Going back to the widget-making company once again, imagine that each widget comes with an operating agreement that has to be renewed each year. This operating agreement makes the widget usable each year that the agreement is renewed. If they don't renew the contract the widget will stop working. Sometimes there is a maintenance contract for the widget that will allow you to use the widget trouble-free for as long as you pay annually or monthly for that maintenance contract. You sold only one widget to the customer, but you continue to get income from the sale of the contracts on a regular basis, possibly indefinitely.

Another great example of residual income is the telephone or cable company. They sell you the service once and then you pay them each and every month to keep that service. The service continues for an indefinite period of time as long as you pay the bill each and every month.

In the dotcom boom, several companies grew big with this type of income. Did you ever hear of AOL? They gave you access to the Internet and all you had to do was have $19.95 withdrawn automatically from your checkbook or credit card each month. How many other services that you use are similar to these? I bet you pay at least 3 residual incomes to big companies each month.

The next income type is investment income. Investment income is just as it sounds, income derived from an investment. Usually this is from a lump sum of money, or a "saved" sum of money, that pays you either a specific or variable amount for either a specific or variable amount of time. A perfect example of this is an annuity. If you remember, with my $25,000,000 winnings, I chose to have an annuity pay me each month. Actually, in my example I chose 4 different annuity contracts to pay me on different weeks of each month, but the fact is that I would receive the $250,000 per year for as long as I lived. It is simply the interest that is paid to me each month from the principal amount of the $4 million. Now that is great investment income.

Another type of investment income is dividends. Dividends are usually paid from a corporation or company that you have ownership in. The dividend is usually based on profit. Part of that profit is distributed to shareholders of the corporation, and that is called a dividend. Sometimes a great business opportunity comes to you; let's say a friend wants to open the widget-making company. He has the plans and the idea, but not the money. You, on the other hand, have the money but no interest in running a widget-making shop. You come to an agreement: you give him your money to open the plant and in return he promises you a payment equal to a percentage of the profit in the form of a dividend. He gets his widget-making shop and you get investment income.

You can also receive dividends from publicly traded stocks. The companies that are traded on the stock exchange may pay a divided to the shareholders. Some of these stocks pay substantially more yield than a typical bank account or mutual fund. If you thought a stock had to go up to make money, well, that isn't exactly correct. If the stock in a certain company is paying a dividend and you are collecting that dividend, then you are always making money from that stock.

This is often why the stock market pundits suggest stocks with high-paying dividends. If you are taking the dividend as income then you are receiving investment income. Even if the stock price goes down, you may still be receiving the original dividend. If you bought a stock for $35 a share and the annual dividend when you bought the stock was $3.5 per share, then you are earning 10% on your original investment. If the stock goes down to $28 a share and the dividend is still $3.5 a year, your divided or yield earnings stay the same at 10% of your investment. The stock market lesson will be for another book, but I wanted to illustrate the power of dividends as an investment income.

Next on the list is growth income. Growth income isn't exactly income as we know it. In a traditional income, and in the examples above, you take the incomes as they are earned or distributed to you. Growth income implies that you are leaving the earned "growth" with the original investment to grow along with the investment.

Let's use real estate for the example. If you have property or a real estate investment, in time the value of the property will increase. For example, if you paid $100,000 for a property, in 5 years it may be worth $150,000. Clearly you didn't take a $10,000 a year income from that property. You just let the value of the property increase each year and then eventually sold it for that $50,000 profit.

This is why real estate rentals are such a powerful investment. They not only produce a residual income, they also produce growth income. Even within a turbulent market, real estate is always a powerful investment. Just make sure you buy smart and don't get in over your head.

Other types of growth income include such vehicles as annuities (during the accumulation phase), savings accounts, mutual funds, stocks, bonds, etc. With these types of investments you put money into them either once or over time and they grow each year or each month, but you don't take the earnings until you sell the investment. Growth income is all about the future. The future often arrives sooner than we think, so make sure you concentrate on the idea of growth income to build yours.

There you have it, the five types of income. You have probably already guessed that there are really only two types of income: active income and passive income. Active income is wages or income that you get paid directly for your time. If you review the rest of the above you will note that residual income, investment income, and growth income are really all forms of passive income. I have separated them for a reason and I suggest that in your mind, you keep them separated as we continue. This is because I discovered something as I made a quick study of the very wealthy. I studied friends who are wealthy and observed famous wealthy people, and I found that the true sign of permanent success is not one source, not even two sources, but a total of seven sources of income.

Donald Trump would be a great example of this theory. I want you to understand that I am really simplifying the explanation of Donald Trump's sources of income to illustrate the seven income streams that he receives. It is also very possible that he is receiving more than seven income streams, but then again, he is Donald Trump and we aren't.

First of all, Trump is a real estate tycoon. That means that one of his passive income sources is the rent paid to him from his real estate. His real estate company collects the rent and manages the properties. They then send him an income check for the profit each and every month for as long as the properties are rented.

Next is his casino operation. From this he makes another passive income from the profits of the casino. Each time someone leaves their hard-earned money at a casino table or slot machine, Trump gets a small percentage of the profit of that money. Remember, following the explanation of passive income, he does not need to be the dealer at the table taking the money; in fact, he could be in another country, just collecting the portion of the winnings that the casino operation pays him.

Donald Trump also does product endorsements, and he gets a residual income each time a commercial or print ad with his likeness is aired or published. He films a commercial or has his photograph taken with a product once and then he gets paid over and over again from that one small investment of his time.

The Apprentice is a hit TV show and from this he earns wages. And I am not talking about $25/ hour wages, but instead really big wages of about $1,000,000 per episode. Nevertheless, they are still wages. He has to be there putting in time for each episode and then he gets paid for his time.

Donald Trump also has a few books on the market. That would be another residual income in the form of royalties. As I explained earlier, royalties come from each and every sale of an item. These royalties are usually paid monthly or quarterly, depending on the contract.

Donald Trump also recently became part of a multi-level marketing system in which the company sells network and communications systems. He receives a small portion of each sale made by the MLM marketing efforts. This is another source of passive income. I will discuss more about multi-level marketing in the next chapter, but for now just consider that a sales force is selling a product and Donald Trump receives an income from each sale of that product.

Finally I am sure that Donald Trump does not put his money under the mattress. He must have growth income from his investments. Of course the real estate alone is a growing investment, but let's focus on the cash investments only for this example. He obviously has money put aside in the stock market and other investment vehicles that earn interest or some other type of return. That interest is compounding in the investment vehicle and it continues to grow.

So let's add it up.

 i. Passive income from real estate
 ii. Passive income from casinos
 iii. Residual income from advertising or product endorsements
 iv. Residual income from books in the form of a royalty
 v. Income or wages from the TV show
 vi. Growth income from investments
 vii. MLM passive income

That would be 3 forms of passive income, 2 forms of residual income, 1 form of wages, and finally, at least 1 form of growth income.

Again, I really simplified things a bit here, but I did it because this book is not here to teach Donald Trump how to be rich; rather it is here for you and me to learn how to become rich.

Now take the income list again and let us examine this theory.

Income types:
 1 Wages, Salary
 2 Passive Income
 3 Residual Income
 4 Investment Income
 5 Growth Income

How many of these incomes did you say you have? I bet it is one, maybe two. I want you to think of the list as a Chinese special menu. You know, the menu where you choose some of the items from a list as your meal. You might choose one of two listed soups, or one of two listed appetizers, or two entrees of a choice of four. You get the idea.

This means that you do not have to use all of the income sources listed, but your lifetime goals should be to have seven total income sources. They can even all be from the same category. Of course, some of the categories are limited by physical constraints. For example, let's say you are making $40,000 a year from your wages income. You now desire to make $100,000 a year. To solve this problem, you may get another job that pays you another $40,000 a year. Of course, this would be a job that would be worked during the hours that you are not working your first full-time job.

You can quickly see that you will run out of time if you had to work two 40-hour-a-week jobs. Besides, you would then still need another part-time job paying you $20,000 a year to reach the $100,000. With 168 hours in a week, you can clearly see that you cannot do this for any length of time without falling down from exhaustion. Also, when would you have the time to enjoy the money you are making anyway? So wages income is again a limited income source. Its limitations are your time, your efforts, and the going rate for your position.

Wages income should eventually become the smallest part of your income. You can clearly see that is has its time limitations as well physical limitations. All of the other types of income have no limitations. Passive income grows as its source grows. Passive income is, in theory, unlimited. For example, your widget-making factory can make and sell more widgets, or maybe introduce better and faster widgets to a new market. As each widget sells, you make a profit in the form of a passive income.

Your residual income also is unlimited; if you have multiple rental properties, you get income from each one. The only limit to this income is how many properties you can buy, and not even Donald Trump owns them all. That leaves you with several opportunities.

Your investment income does have some limitations. The limitations are based on your capitol investment and risk factors. If you are a conservative investor and stay with fixed funds, your income may be lower than someone collecting investment income from a higher-risk fund. Of course with the conservative fund you have little risk of losing your income or original investment amount, whereas the high-risk funds can cause you to lose some or all of your entire principal, therefore losing the investment income.

Finally, growth income is also limited to the amount of capitol you can put aside in a lump sum or installments. Remember the 10% of your income you are putting aside? That is the first source for your growth income. Invest that money wisely and it will grow in ways you could not imagine, and more quickly than you think.

So there you have it, your goal is seven sources of income from the 5 types listed. You can use them all or you can pick and choose from the list, using some of them several times.

I know what you are thinking: "I am having trouble with my one source of income, my job! How am I going to start concentrating on six more sources?" First, take a deep breath and realize that this will not and cannot happen overnight. It will take planning and execution of ideas to get there. In the next chapter I will discuss various business opportunities and ideas for your other sources of income.

Finally, I also want to mention that you are always going to eventually live on passive income. When you retire, either by choice or by force, you will be collecting some form of passive income. This passive income will probably be in the form of Social Security. (I am not one of those who thinks

Social Security won't be there when I retire, but I am doing whatever I can to make sure it is not my only source of income, just in case.)

Other sources of income at retirement may include a pension or other retirement program in place by your employer. If you were a good saver then you may have an IRA that is now paying you an income. All of these are forms of residual income. The interesting part about this is that, at retirement, people start utilizing residual income and they don't even understand or realize that they could have had residual income for many years before retirement. Some retirees have three sources of income: Social Security, pension, and an investment income such as an IRA or annuity. While they were employees they had one source; after retirement they have three sources. That should make you think!

Did you ever wonder why some people can do all of the things they always wanted to do after they retire? It is because they are utilizing the power of multiple sources of income. Why do they wait until they are older? Is it ignorance, fear, or just mediocrity?

We must find ways to create and utilize the other income sources while we are young enough to really enjoy them. The other sources of income will create freedom, security, and wealth. Start thinking about residual income sources. Stop concentrating on wages income.

Now for my next set of lottery numbers.

Remember to read them out loud for me!

4 5 9 10 25 Powerball 11

Chapter 13

Don't Make a Living, Make a Life.

For most Americans, every day is the same old tired routine. Get up, take a shower, eat breakfast, get in the car, go to work, then at the end of the week you get a paycheck, you struggle to pay your bills, and then do it all over again. They call this *making a living.* It is no wonder that illnesses like stress, heart attacks, and depression are running wild in our society. This is no way to make a complex organism like a human happy! We have desires and dreams that we should be working on fulfilling. What dream are we fulfilling with the routine of working for someone? Is it the dream of being a slave, or being owned by your employer? Or maybe it is the dream of being a mouse in maze, always traveling the same road to the same destination, getting the same piece of cheese, a paycheck, at the end of the week. Maybe you are a true missionary and really enjoy helping to build the dreams of the company owner. Or, if you work for a big public corporation, you really enjoy building the company for the benefit of the stockholders. Honestly, if you said yes to any of these, you need to put the book down and seek counseling because you are under the delusion that you are worthless. *That was harsh and I hope you aren't insulted, but it is true!*

Now it is time to decide how you are going to live your life. Are you going to be that mouse in the maze, or are you going to be the one who places the cheese at the end? Are your dreams going to be fulfilled, or are you going to make someone else's dreams come true? Are you going to be the one who makes the stockholders rich, or are you going to be the stockholder benefiting from all the other mice in the maze?

If you have decided to stay a mouse, then there is nothing in this book that can help you and you have read it just for entertainment. If you decide to be the cheese master, the stockholder or the company owner, then read on for some ideas that may just help.

By now you should have a clear picture in your mind of your dreams and desires. If you took my advice, you have written them down, they are placed where you can see them, and you are reading them every day. In order to manifest your dreams, you are going to need a plan. Everyone's plans are different, so I hope to enlighten you about some of the concepts that are available to you as you start to build your seven sources of income. Your imagination will help guide you as you read the various ideas listed. You should try to imagine yourself in each situation and how YOU can do any or all of the ideas listed. You should also not limit yourself to the ideas listed, because frankly there is no limit to the possibilities of how to earn both passive and active incomes.

A quick reminder of the income types:

1.   Wages, Salary is a limited and active income
2.   Passive Income is an inactive and unlimited income
3.   Residual Income is a form of passive income
4.   Investment Income is another form of passive income
5.   Growth Income is income that grows but is not or cannot be utilized immediately

If you recall, I stated that wages income is just a temporary income; however, it is important that you have wages income while you are building your other sources. This is truly the fastest income to acquire, and usually with this income comes other benefits like health insurance paid or partially paid by your employer. You may need these benefits as you get started on your journey. Eventually you will be able to afford your own benefits as well as everything else you want and need.

First, I would like to discuss how to truly maximize your wages income as an employee. Or simply, *get paid what you are worth!* Do you remember the widget-making factory and the producer who produced more widgets? Well, if he continued to be paid the same wages as the rest of the lower-producing widget makers, I concluded that he would probably not continue producing at the current rate for long. However, what if he received a bonus for creating widgets above the average productivity? Do you think that might motivate the worker to continue his current higher productivity? In fact it might also motivate some of the other low-producing widget makers to produce more if they knew a bonus was waiting for them when they reached a certain number as well.

How about the salespeople selling the widgets; would they have any incentive to sell more widgets if they received the same pay as someone who sold fewer widgets? Again, what if they received a bonus for selling a higher amount of widgets? Maybe they could receive a commission on each and every widget they sold. This would certainly make the higher producer more income. These are some of the types of wages income I will discuss and that you should concentrate on.

The simplest form of wages income is based on an hourly rate. This simply means that if you work an hour, you get an hour's pay. No matter how productive or unproductive you are, if your hourly wage is $12 an hour, you can rest assured that you will get your $12-an-hour pay in your next pay cycle. This is easy and really needs no explanation. So let's try a different hourly approach.

I have a friend named Tom who is in the auto body shop business. Tom is a car painter. When someone wrecks their car, the body work gets repaired by someone in the body department of the auto body shop and then Tom paints the car.

According to the rules of how insurance payments work, the shop can bill the insurance company for a certain amount of hours for each part of the car that is to be painted. This amount of hours is decided in advance by the insurance companies and is printed in a book for the body shop and insurance adjuster to use as guidelines for the estimate for the repair.

For example, if a car needs the front fender painted and the book says it will take 4.5 hours to prep and paint that fender, then Tom's department can be paid the prevailing rate per hour for 4.5 hours no matter how long it takes. That means that whether Tom takes 6 hours to prep and paint the car or 2 hours to prep and paint the car, he will receive exactly the same amount of payment for the work: 4.5 hours of payment. This allows Tom to actually work and get paid for 80 hours in a 40 hour work week!

Let me run that by you in a simpler explanation. If Tom paints all of his cars in half the time printed in the cost book, then his department can get paid for 80 hours of work instead of 40 hours of work. This means Tom essentially worked 80 hours in a 40 hour work week.

My friend Tom is smart. He works on what they call a flat rate hourly pay. That means that he gets paid the billable hours, not the actual work hours. Think about it; if Tom makes $25 an hour and was paid on the actual 40 hours, he would get $1000/week for his work. Well, Tom gets $25/hour for each billable hour instead, so if he bills 80 hours and works 40 hours (which he usually does) then he makes $2000 a week, double his pay!

However, there is a catch. Tom is not responsible for bringing work into the shop. That means when the shop is slow, Tom may only be able to bill 30 hours for a 40 hour work week, therefore only bringing home $800 for that week. This means that Tom is truly paid for his efforts. His wages salary is optimized by his hard work ethic and desire to build a better life for his family. Flat rate hourly work is truly one way to optimize wages income. There are other types of industries that will also pay you flat rate hourly. If you like this type of pay, you should seek out these industries for your wages income.

The next way to earn your worth in wages is through commission sales. Did you know that some of the highest paid people in America are salespeople? It is true! Salespeople in fact have unlimited earning potential. Most work on either little or no base income. That means that if they don't sell, they make little or no income. But if they are really good at it they can literally make millions.

If you decide to take a position in sales, here is some advice. Always ask the hiring manager or owner of the company you are interviewing with, "What does the highest paid person in the company make per year as a salesperson?" This question will help determine your true earnings potential. Think about it: if you want to make $200,000 per year selling widgets, and the top salesperson only makes $100,000, why would you think that you will outsell him by 100%? This is highly unlikely indeed. It also may mean that the desire for the product the company is selling may not be high enough for you to reach your goals, thus making another company or product a better choice for you.

For me, when I take a sales position, I want to be sure the current top earner is making at least 25% more than I want to make. I do this because I know that it may take a while to get to the top, and before I reach it I want to be sure that I can earn at or close to my earning needs.

Bonuses and overrides are another way to maximize wage earnings. These types of positions are usually managerial positions. The manager will receive a passive income for each unit of production of the people he manages. For example, if the workers make more widgets or the salespeople sell more widgets, the manager will receive extra pay. Overrides usually mean that for each widget produced or sold the manager makes a portion of the profit. A bonus usually implies that a certain amount of production must be reached before any extra money is earned.

The final type of wages income to discuss is a sharing of the profits of the company, or, as it is referred to, "profit sharing." Imagine how hard you would work for a company if you knew that you received a percentage of each dollar earned by that company. Profit is usually defined by gross income minus expenses. This is also referred to as P&L income, or profit and loss income. The disadvantage to this type of income is that sometimes the weakest producer will benefit from the efforts of the higher producer. This is because the profit sharing is usually distributed to all of the employees in that class. It is true that with seniority or higher pay an employee may get higher profit sharing pieces, but still, the lowest producer will always get something. If you work hard and produce well, this is another great way to maximize your wages income.

There are certainly other ways to maximize wages income, but in order for you to earn what you are truly worth, your income should always be based on your contribution to your company. This will make you more income as well as making the company that employs you more profitable. If your company allows for this type of income, you should speak with the supervisor or owner about how you can change your income to any of the listed types. If not, you should immediately seek out employment that will allow you to maximize your wages income.

The list, once again, is as follows:

1. Flat hourly rate
2. Commission
3. Override
4. Bonus
5. Profit sharing or P&L income

Next, it's time to start thinking about passive income sources. Passive income, as discussed in the last chapter, can come from many places and is virtually unlimited. I want to touch on a few ideas that may get your imagination working for you to start earning passive income.

Nothing beats real estate for passive income. "Rent" is the name of the passive income from real estate. To be successful in real estate you must buy properties with stable rent, predictable turnover, and, of course, positive cash flow. Without positive cash flow, not only will you not have residual income, you will actually have a residual expense.

I could probably write a book on real estate investing, but for this book, I would like to review some basics in finding the right property for you. I have found that most real estate agents do not have a clue as to which properties they should show a potential investor. If you choose to use a real estate agent, be sure you understand and adhere to the following criteria before looking for any properties.

The first is a simple rule of thumb that usually works. The monthly rent should be no less than 1% of the purchase price of the property. For example, if you can get rent of $1000 per month, you should pay no more than $100,000 for the property. Usually the mortgage, taxes, insurance and other fees will be about $800 for a $100,000 property; therefore, you will make about $200 a month.

Here is another rule of thumb that is also important; you should always try to make at least $200 per month profit from all rental units. Never buy a property for pure rental income unless you are making at least $200 a month in positive cash flow.   The following is a simple spreadsheet to determine if your real estate rental will be profitable. This spreadsheet will help you with the "math" only. Be sure you do all of the due diligence before buying a property. You can find a working copy of this spreadsheet which will allow you put in your actual numbers at the book website www.25milliondollarmasterminds.com.

Simple spreadsheet for profit
Monthly numbers
(leave empty if tenant is paying or not applicable)

Rent totals	$1000
Mortgage	$665
Taxes	$100
Insurance	$50
Water	$25
Repairs	$25
Gas	0
Heating oil	0
Vacancy % (use 5% unless you have actual)	5%
Advertising	$25
Total Expenses	$773
Vacancy loss	$55
Profit	$217

This is an example of a $100,000 property with an 80% mortgage at an interest rate of 7%. You should always try to put 20% or more down on a real estate property investment. This will help you to avoid trouble later and it will also make it easier for the bank to approve your loan. Twenty percent down also helps you to avoid extra fees like PMI. PMI is Private Mortgage Insurance that you pay for to protect the bank from you defaulting on the loan. Usually PMI will cost you about $100 or more for the above example. You should check with your bank to find out the exact amount it will cost. With the PMI it is clear that this example would have a less desirable cash flow making it less profitable. .

In the example I have entered all of the facts for the property. The vacancy rate is something that is not a predictable factor if you do not own the property over a long period of time or have accurate vacancy records. This makes a prediction difficult, so a good default is 5%. This will help you put away some profit for a time where the property is empty and you are not collecting rent. Advertising is also a factor only when the property is empty. You will need to advertise in local papers or on the Internet for viable tenants, so if you put away a small amount from your rent each month, you will be well prepared to pay for the advertising.

Sometimes it may be easier to turn the property over to a rental management company. These companies usually charge 10% of the collected rent as a fee and they will make sure that the property is occupied at their expense. Management companies also will be the first contact for your tenants if anything needs attention. Some real estate investors do not want to be bothered with the "toilet overflowing" or "no heat" calls, so they use the management companies to manage these problems. The management company will usually have a crew or a select team of sub-contractors to make repairs. The management company will then bill you for any repairs. You should know that most management companies add a fee to the bill as well. Usually this is about 5-10% of the cost of the repair.

If you choose a management company, be sure that they are familiar with the area where your property is located. If they are not familiar with the area then they usually will not be familiar with the various unique situations that come up in that area. You may find that an unfamiliar company may charge less, but this is certainly no place to be *penny wise and pound foolish.*

If you own a property in another state, or the property is more than a 45 minute trip, I highly recommend a management company. You clearly cannot manage a property that is far away. Your tenants will also not be happy when you take more than an hour just to look at a problem. If you choose to use a management company, make sure you add the fee as an expense on your spreadsheet before you decide to buy a property.

Real estate is a great investment for another reason as well. Equity is the part of the property that you actually can call an asset. Equity grows in your property every time you make a payment of principal to your loan. That means that if your property never goes up in value, you will have made about 400% profit after your loan is paid off.

Let me explain using the same $100,000 property. Start with the example of putting 20% down, or $20,000 on a $100,000 property. If you make all of the payments, usually 30 years' worth, and assuming the property never increases in value, then you own a $100,000 asset clear and free after the mortgage is paid in full.

If your tenants have been paying you, then technically they have been paying your mortgage. Not only did your initial $20,000 grow to $100,000, but you also made about $200 per month each month. This again assumes that you never raise the rent for the entire 30 years. That means that you made $80,000 from the initial investment of $20,000, and you made about $2400 a year for 30 years, or another $72,000, over that time.

Remember, this is if you never raise the rent and if the property never goes up in value. However, both of those scenarios are highly unlikely. Most real estate goes up in value and you will certainly raise the rent every few years. This is why real estate is one of the best investments for passive income as well as growth income.

Another way to gain a passive income is to own your own business. Of course, if you truly want to own a business that pays passive income then you need either employees or a machine that does all of the work for you. I recently saw a kiosk in the mall that dispensed acne medication. I truly thought this was brilliant. You load up the machine with product and then it, the machine, does all the work. The machine takes both cash and credit cards and then the product drops out of a door at the bottom. The owner never needs to be there and there are no employees or any of the hassles associated with a store. As a matter of fact the machine was relatively small and I bet they paid a mere fraction of rent compared to any other store in the mall.

This concept has been around for years in vending machines that dispense soda and candy. Some even dispense food, such as sandwiches, but I bet those companies do not make anywhere near the profit of this acne medication vending machine. Vending machines will certainly prove to be a great way of making passive income. They are always there and always at work. If you need employees to distribute a product, then you must concern yourself with the legal issues of payroll, taxes, unemployment insurance, and benefits. Honestly, it is actually pretty easy once you learn how, and I recommend a payroll processing company to help keep it all legal and on time.

Now that you have a distribution system for your product, either man or machine, it is time to decide what your product will be. This is where your imagination and desires come in. There are all types of products you can sell and the list is literally unlimited. These are just a tiny fraction of the items you can sell to the average consumer: household goods, auto goods, telecommunication devices such as cell phones, computer equipment, food, electronics, appliances, office supplies, insurance or financial services, books, specialty items, clothing, tools, and so many more. You could even sell wholesale as a distributor to other people trying to sell items. With a little research you will find all of the suppliers you need to sell your product to your target consumer.

Now you need to decide if you are going sell at a fixed location, such as a store, or via other methods, such as the Internet. I have a few friends who make a nice living selling collectables, and their distribution system is eBay. How easy is that? All they do is take pictures and post them on eBay to sell the items.

If you choose a store, then be sure to do the research on your location and your product. Make sure that the product will have a demand in that area and that your competition hasn't already taken most of the market share.

A few things to do when you own a store is to make sure you are operating within the rules and laws of your state. A few common things to remember are sales tax, operating licenses (if needed), and payroll taxes. I also recommend that with any business you incorporate, to keep you removed from the liability of anything that goes wrong. Seek an attorney who is familiar with Limited Liability Corporations (LLC), S corporations, and sole proprietorships. In most cases they will advise you to go the route of an LLC. Even though I am not an attorney or an accountant, I can tell you never to open up any business without one of these structures in place.

If you open a business without any experience you will make many mistakes. Most people do not understand basic business and marketing techniques, and this is why most businesses fail in the first 3 years. To open a "virgin business" takes a small investment, usually under $35,000, before even buying the product you intend to sell. This money is usually spent on rent, security deposits, retrofitting a location, legal fees, and operating expenses before you even open the doors. If you are not covering your monthly expenses with sales, then you also will need some money to keep the doors open as you work up to a profit. You should anticipate a one year period before you break even on a monthly basis, so you need to keep a fund available to pay the bills until the profits build up. All of this is probably another $25,000. If your product is sound and you did your homework, then soon after the first year you should start making a reasonable monthly profit. Remember that reasonable profit does not mean you are getting rich; on the contrary, you will probably be bringing home close to or even less than your employees. It takes time for a business to grow and make the money you expect.

If you want a head start, then a franchise may be the business for you. Franchises offer you all of the pluses of owning your own business and they help lower the downside risk. Franchises are well established businesses, usually with a well established business model. They also offer you training and local advertising to help make your business profitable quickly.

Most people think of food franchises, such as McDonald's or Subway; however, there are franchises in just about every type of business available. I knew a guy who owned a Party Center franchise. Actually, over time he owned over ten stores in the area. His franchise sold party goods, such as balloons, paper plates, wrapping paper, and other party favors. The franchise even sold Halloween costumes during September and October. He was an accountant by trade and almost never went into the stores. He had managers and other staff run the stores for him. Those stores created a fantastic residual income for him.

Franchises do, however, have a higher start-up cost. Usually franchise fees range anywhere from $10,000 to over $1,000,000. This fee is just to buy the privilege of using the name and selling the product. The advantage is the training, support, and brand recognition you will get for your initial franchise fee.

The franchise company also takes a percentage of your sales each month as an ongoing monthly fee. This fee is usually up to 10% of your gross receipts for the month or quarter. As you can see, owning a franchise can cost a lot of money. As a matter of fact, most franchises want you to have a certain net worth before they will even consider taking you on as a franchise owner. They do this to make sure that you have the personal reserves to keep your business flowing in bad times. Franchises sell all types of products and services. I have a friend doing quite well with a Harley Davidson franchise and another with a Ford franchise. These are very expensive franchised companies, but I can see the rewards gained by the owners.

Other smaller franchises include weight loss companies, convenience stores, ice cream stores, wireless phone services, various food outlets, bathroom and kitchen remodeling, and so many more. There are franchises for just about every type of business. Something you should keep in mind is that you are not guaranteed a profit, or guaranteed to be a success, unless you work hard and do a lot of research before you start.

I usually use a pretzel franchise as an example for determining whether a franchise will be successful. I have a friend who, when the pretzel companies were opening everywhere, bought the exclusive rights for a pretzel franchise in the small town where she resides. She paid $40,000 just for the right to open the store in this specific town. This $40,000 paid for nothing else. Not the retrofit, the legal council, the materials—nothing but the right to open the store. To open the store she would also have to buy the pretzel oven as well as other materials from the franchise. After the security deposit, retrofit, and other materials, she determined she would need another $75,000 just to open.

She was trying to determine what to do. She had already bought the rights and spent her $40,000. The question was, should she spend the rest and actually open the store? The other catch was that her right to open the store expired two years after her contract. That means that if she didn't open the store before the 2 years expired, then the franchise company could sell the right to someone else and remove her from the franchise without a refund to her.

She was scrambling for advice from several people and came to me. I broke it down very simply. I said, "Let's use the 'pretzel formula' to determine your possible success." I explained that if the average pretzel sells for $1, then you need to sell 1500 pretzels a month to make the rent (the rent in the area was about $1500/month). You then need to sell about 400 pretzels to pay the utilities and another 200 pretzels to pay for insurance. If you have employees, then you will need to sell about 8 pretzels per hour per employee just to pay them, or about 1200 pretzels per month per employee. She felt she needed at least 2 employees for a total of 2400 pretzels. I asked if she needed a loan and she said yes. The loan payment was about another 700 pretzels a month. That means that she needed to sell about 5000 pretzels a month. This was before factoring in the cost to make the pretzels or the monthly franchise fee. That would probably cost another 1500 pretzels for a total of 6500 pretzels a month, just to break even. Every pretzel sold over 6500 a month would begin to give her a profit. I looked at her and asked, "Are you going to sell at least 6500 pretzels a month?" After she examined the foot traffic in the town, she felt she could not sell that many and decided against it.

About a month after her 2 year expiration date, a sign went up in a window in a store on the street on which she had wanted to open. You guessed it: "Coming Soon, Pretzels." The store opened shortly after and we found out that the owner was actually paying over $3000 in rent, double the amount my friend was thinking she would have to pay. We didn't even ask about the other bills. Sure enough, he threw in the towel after just 3 months because he wasn't selling anywhere near the 8000 pretzels he needed to sell.

I knew another friend who bought a traveling dog-grooming franchise. He paid about $25,000 for the rights to the franchise, another $40,000 each for two fully equipped trucks, and hired 2 people to help. On average the price for a grooming was $75 per dog. That means in order to break even (before gas, employees, taxes, and insurance) he would need to groom 1400 dogs. If he wanted to break even in 2 years, he would need to groom about 14 dogs per week. If you add the employees, he would probably need to double that to cover the payroll. That means that if you can groom each dog once a month, and get the highly unlikely 100% repeat business, then you need about 120 steady clients. That also means you are grooming 120 dogs per month just to break even! So the pretzel formula applied here means that on a five day work schedule, they needed to groom about 3 dogs per day per truck every day in a 5 day work week. I guess you can understand why they failed at this business.

My advice to you, if you decide to open a franchise or in fact any business, is to use the pretzel formula before you plunk down a large sum of money. Simply ask yourself, "How many of the item or items do I need to sell to pay my bills?" If it is pretzels, or candy, or a dog-grooming franchise, how many sales or services do you need just to pay the bills? Franchises do work, but they require a lot of work. If you do the math and have the money to buy into a franchise, then it may be the path for you.

What if you don't have a few ten thousand dollars or more to buy a franchise? Another great type of business ownership is Multi-Level-Marketing, sometimes called Network Marketing. Multi-Level-Marketing, or MLM, is often put into the category of the term "pyramid scheme." I assure you that if you are considering an MLM company that has been in business for a while, you are not considering any type of scheme.

MLM companies are truly the type of business ownership for the average person who has little or no start-up money. The average MLM costs about $100 for what would be considered the franchise fee. In MLM, you make commissions on the products you sell and overrides on all of the people whom you bring into the MLM. A MLM will truly give you a great passive income from the people you bring into the business.

Imagine you indeed had a successful pretzel franchise store. Your friend, seeing your great success, decided he wanted to open a store like yours in another area. You, being a good friend, introduce him to your franchise salesperson and he signs up. Sure enough his store is successful. So what do you get? Well, the franchise salesperson may give you baseball tickets as a "thank you" or maybe a referral fee of $500, but really all you got was the satisfaction of helping your friend.

Now imagine that the franchise company had a program in place that gave you 30% percent of all of your friend's profits because you referred him. They also give him 30% of all the profits from any store that he introduces a friend to. Along with that, the referral overrides in this pretzel store franchise allow you to make 10% of the profits from the people your friend is making 30% on. The program is so great that it will even give you 5% of the profit from any friends that your friend's friend brings in. Also, if that friend brings in someone you will get 3% of those profits. Imagine if the pretzel company will allow you to get an override up to 6 levels deep! This is the definition and magic of Multi-Level-Marketing.

MLM companies service so many different products and services. Some of the more popular ones are Amway, Herbalife, Tupperware, Avon, and Mary Kay. There is even an MLM called Primerica that sells financial services such as annuities and life insurance. If you like what you have read in this book regarding money and you would like to help people with these ideas, then

Primerica may be the MLM for you. There is also a new MLM that also uses some of the same behavioral modification concepts describe in this book. Its purpose is to help people stop smoking, lose weight, control diabetes or have less stress. It is called Focus My Health.

The problem with people who join MLM's is they think they do not have to work to make money. Just like any business, you need to devote time and effort to the business. If you owned the pretzel store and only opened 3 days a week for 3 hours, you certainly wouldn't make any money and would soon be out of business. It is the same with an MLM business.

If you work at the business, both selling the product and recruiting people into the business, your income is virtually unlimited. You usually need to make only one sale to break even on the franchise fee and you can usually use the product you are selling anyway, so the first sale, the break-even sale, is easy.

Do you remember the fear/desire number line? The fear is usually what makes people fail in these types of businesses. The excuses that the fear brings sound something like these: "I don't want to bother my friends," "I just want to sell products, not recruit," "My friend says this is a pyramid scheme," "Only the people at the top make any money," and so on. If people have the desire then the fear is easy to overcome. Do you have the desire for a virtually unlimited passive income with little start-up cost? If you said "yes" then MLM may be for you.

By the way, I want to address the last fear, "only the people at the top make any money." The very nature of MLMs says that you are always at the top. You can collect overrides (passive income) from only 6 levels below you by law. The people at the top can collect overrides from only 6 levels below them. The laws are very clear for MLMs and they make it so that everyone, the first person in or the person who signs up 20 years later, has exactly the same chance of making the same unlimited income. If you decide to go into an MLM, make sure it is a product you can believe in; that way your heart will be in it and your drive for success will be greater.

Another thing to consider with MLMs is the people above you, also known as your "up-line." These people can truly make the difference for your success. All MLMs, like all businesses, have serious hard-working people and not so serious hard-working people. If your up-line has no organization or does not have weekly meetings, then you should consider a different person to sponsor you into a different up-line. Don't give up on the company; just consider your up-line carefully.

MLMs also offer great training and what I call "Rah Rah" sessions. If you have a good up-line, your free "Rah Rah" sessions are probably worth thousands of dollars in motivational seminars. These meetings are truly motivational and can help you in a variety of areas in your life. The sales skills taught in these meetings are usually very informative as well. So not only do you get an opportunity for about $100, you also get a lifetime subscription to motivational meetings. All you need to do is show up for the weekly or bi-weekly meetings.

If you are interested in MLMs, simply do a Google search with the keywords MLM and your product (i.e., "MLM cosmetics"). You can also go to the www.25milliondollarmasterminds.com website to request information on specific MLM's.

Other ways of earning passive income will come to you as you explore your desires. You may want to be a writer or a public speaker like me. You may want to invent a new product or improve on a product. There are so many opportunities, and if you let your imagination take you to these new ideas, they will unfold in front of you like a butterfly emerging from a cocoon.

The last income to talk about is growth income. As I explained, growth income is income that you cannot or will not receive immediately. Real estate, as explained earlier, is a great method for earning growth income. As the saying goes, "Don't wait to buy real estate; buy real estate and wait."

Other types of growth income are usually cash investment types. A simple savings account or a bank CD is a form of growth income. You deposit a certain amount of money and at the end of a certain period of time, you get your money back, plus interest.

Growth income can be conservative or risky. Conservative growth types would include the bank savings or CDs. The problem with this type of income is that it will grow very slowly. The advantage, of course, is that you will never lose your principal. Stocks, bonds, and mutual funds are more risky because you can lose your principal amount. The advantage is that the earnings can be very high. There is a formula referred to as the "rule of 72." This formula will help you determine how many years it will take to double your initial investment at a given interest rate.

The formula is: **Years to Double = 72/interest rate.**

That simply means that if you have a 5% interest rate you can determine that it will take 14.4 years to double your investment. If you have a 10% interest rate, it will take you 7.2 years to double your investment. As you can see, the better the interest rate the sooner you will double your money.

The stock market may be a place for you to double your money quickly. I will warn you that if you are not familiar with terms like P/E multiple, Beta, call options, put options, fundamental analysis, technical analysis, dividends, and other pertinent stock market concepts, your chances of success in the stock market are slim to none. If you want to invest in any risky investment options like stocks, bonds, or mutual funds, you have two choices. Either get a good advisor, or learn these terms and investment strategies. There are many courses on the latter and I recommend them before you start investing your hard-earned money.

As for the rule of 72, you need to ask yourself, "At your age, how many double opportunities do you have left before you retire or need the money?" Let's say you are 40 years old and you want to retire at 60. If you have saved $100,000 and need to have $400,000 to retire, then you need to double this money twice in 20 years. If you use the formula **Years to Double= 72/ interest rate** then you will need to get an interest rate of 7.2% to reach this goal. At 7.2% you have only 2 doubling periods to make it to 60. If you want more money at age 60 you will need a higher interest rate. If you can't get a higher interest rate, well, then you have to wait longer to use the money.

There are many ways to obtain the seven sources of incomes from the five types of incomes. Concentrate on one income at a time, taking the time to decide how you are going to do it. You should start by improving your wages income first. You should already have started to put away your 10% into your growth income fund or funds. Now start to work on the other incomes. It will take time, but if you build them one by one, you will have truly built a better life for yourself and your family.

Now for my next set of lottery numbers.

Remember to read them out loud!

9 14 26 29 39 Powerball 11

Chapter 14

Happiness is...

If I could only win the lottery, I would be so happy! I have heard this from so many people. They say it in passing; they say it in wishes, they even say it in prayer. If we already concluded that many or most people who win the lottery are miserable, then why is that people believe that it will make them happier? Jim Carey once said, *"I wish everyone could get rich and famous and everything they ever dreamed of so they can see that's not the answer.*[1]

How many times have you heard the expression "money doesn't buy you happiness"? Does that mean poverty brings you happiness? I don't think so. I would imagine that people with even a small amount of money are generally happier than people who have absolutely no money. That doesn't mean that they can literally go into a store and buy happiness. How great would it be if they could? They would say to the person behind the happiness counter, "I will take ten pounds of happiness today." The very rich would say, "Have a ton of happiness delivered to my mansion on Elm Street," so I guess the poor person would say, "All I can afford is an ounce of happiness this week; my husband is still out of work."

There might even be charities set up where the people with too much happiness can donate a small piece of happiness to the poor. Or maybe you could have "rollover happiness" that lets you use your unused happiness the next day or month if you need it, something like the popular cell phone company has. No, money truly cannot buy happiness.

If anything worth having costs something, then how much does happiness cost? Like most people, you probably answered "nothing." Is this really true? I posted this question on some blogs and I mostly received the same answer. "It costs nothing." Every once in a while I read some interesting answers; one read something like this:

me + motorcycle = happiness
wind hitting face= happiness
family + friends= happiness

So I asked this person, if the motorcycle is involved, then doesn't the cost of the motorcycle need to be included in the cost of happiness?

Some of the other unique answers were about people who lived with tragedy. One person has a wife who is disabled and he recently had open heart surgery, but he insists he is happy. I have met this person and I truly believe he is happy.

This prompted further questions, and the next was, "If some people go through disasters and can say that they are generally happy and others can go through the same or not even as bad disasters and they are miserable all the time, what is the difference?"

The answers were generally the same: attitude. Of course, I had to ask, "If happiness comes from attitude, then can you buy attitude or can you pay someone to help you change your attitude?"

Then my final two questions were: "On a scale of 1-10, how happy would you be if you won $25 million dollars in the lottery?", and "On the same scale, how happy are you now?" This question perplexed everyone.

So I searched for happiness on the Internet, and these are some of the many quotes on happiness that I found: 2

> True happiness is not attained through self-gratification, but through fidelity to a worthy purpose.
> Helen Keller

> Happiness is contagious...when you reflect happiness, then all others around you catch the happy bug and are happy, too.
> Jennifer Leese

> A happy person is not a person in a certain set of circumstances, but rather a person with a certain set of attitudes.
> Hugh Downs

> Happiness is the meaning and the purpose of life, the whole aim and end of human existence.
> Aristotle

> Happiness ain't a thing in itself--it's only a contrast with something that ain't pleasant.
> Mark Twain

Happiness comes only from appreciating what you have right now. You can even be happy by appreciating your troubles because they are helping to build your character.

Harriet Meyerson

Happiness is mostly a by-product of doing what makes us feel fulfilled.

Dr. Benjamin Spock

Thousands of candles can be lighted from a single candle, And the life of the candle will not be shortened. Happiness never decreases by being shared.

Buddha

Happiness: An agreeable sensation arising from contemplating the misery of another.

Ambrose Bierce

There is no cosmetic for beauty like happiness.

Countess of Blessington

Happiness is not merely a life lived by accumulating moments of pleasure. On the contrary, happiness is a long lasting enduring enjoyment of life, it is being in love with living. It is your reward for achieving a good character and personal rational values in life. Some important values are a productive career, romance, friendship and hobbies.

Dr. Ellen Kenner.

Happiness is living in a state of freely choosing to create and exchange one's rational values with others.

John Roberts

Happiness is a thing to be practiced, like the violin.

John Lubbock

To be truly happy and contented, you must let go of what it means to be happy or content.

Confucius

The true way to render ourselves happy is to love our work and find in it our pleasure.

Francoise de Motteville

Happiness is something you get as a by-product in the process of making something else.

Aldous Huxley

Happiness is when your mind is thinking through your heart.
Judi Singleton

Happiness can be defined, in part at least, as the fruit of the desire and ability to sacrifice what we want now for what we want eventually.
Stephen Covey

Finding happiness is like finding yourself. You don't find happiness, you make happiness. You choose happiness. Self-actualization is a process of discovering who you are, who you want to be and paving the way to happiness by doing what brings YOU the most meaning and contentment to your life over the long run.
, The Happy Guy. David Leonhardt, also has a website called thehappyguy.com, with these lines published

Of course, there is the Beatles song "Happiness is a Warm Gun."
And the list went on and on and on....

As I explored it, I found that there are over 19 million hits on the words "Happiness is" in a Google search. I have come to the conclusion that happiness is indefinable! Or maybe not indefinable, but defined differently for each and every one of us. Happiness is truly an anomaly for us to define as individuals.

Even the Constitution says, "We hold these truths to be self-evident, that all men are created equal, that they are endowed by their Creator with certain unalienable rights, that among these are life, liberty and the pursuit of happiness."

If our Constitution says we have the right to pursue happiness, then shouldn't happiness be something we can define?

According to Wikipedia, "happy" is defined as an emotion that you feel when you find beauty and hope in the world around you. "Ness" is defined as *the state of, or condition of being something e.g., awkwardness = the state of being awkward.* That means happiness is the state of being happy!

Wikipedia goes on to say happiness *can also be caused by someone being kind to you or offering you a compliment. It usually means that you are pleased with yourself as a person and find meaning in your existence.*

With all this in mind, how do we achieve this happiness state?

As I wrote earlier, someone suggested "attitude." This, and our thought patterns, are what I believe can lead to true happiness.

While I was contemplating this chapter, I noticed something interesting on day that I was fighting with an insurance company to pay a claim on a stolen vehicle. I had to state my story over and over to several people in the claims department of the insurance company and, frankly, I was getting a bit frustrated. I have to admit they were very polite, but they also appeared to be very incompetent. I had to call them over and over, 7 days in a row, before I would even get someone who could find the claim information that I gave each day in each call. It still is not resolved, but that is not the point of this story.

The point of this story is not to complain about the poor service I had with the claim, but rather to tell you what happened through a few of those days. I noticed something several times during those days of calling the insurance company. What I noticed was even a bit strange. I noticed my thoughts would often go to places where I felt there to be an injustice in the past. Maybe I would think about someone who owed me money from twenty years ago, or maybe a business deal that went bad and how I wished I had pursued the other party to make it right. I even thought about the judge's decision in my divorce case twenty years ago. Boy, were those bad thoughts.

I then noticed that I was yelling at every discourteous driver that day. I was a bit intolerant and impatient at times. When I realized what was happening, I came to the conclusion that my mind had opened up some memory files triggered by the frustration of having to fight with the insurance company. This was truly amazing to me. A phone conversation at about 10 am caused bad thoughts as late as 6 pm that evening. As a matter of fact, I probably wouldn't have made the connection if I wasn't also thinking about the information for this chapter on happiness.

Then something else happened. I thought about how I felt at the moment and realized that I wasn't mad or upset, I was just sort of unhappy. I wasn't depressed, nor was I sad or even down, I was simply unhappy. At that moment I laughed at myself out loud and then realized that I could make myself think about something that made me happy. Guess what, it worked!

Next I began to think about the fact that if I wasn't sad or mad or depressed, it must mean that all of these things are separate. Or simply put, I believe you can be happy and sad and mad and depressed all at once. Think about it, have you ever consoled someone who was sad and they laughed at a joke you made? Have you ever seen someone who was depressed break into a smile? How about someone mad who does a kind gesture for someone else, such as giving up a seat on the train to someone elderly or disabled? I would imagine that you are currently thinking of times this phenomenon has happened to you. You were angry but kind, you were depressed but laughed, you were sad but smiled.

This can only mean that these, and all of our emotions, are completely separate and, if they could be measured, would be measured separately. If we could actually measure them it would probably be something like this (the higher the number the more intense the emotion):

Happy Scale	1<>2<>3<>4<>5<>6<>7<>8<>9<>10
Sad Scale	1<>2<>3<>4<>5<>6<>7<>8<>9<>10
Depressed Scale	1<>2<>3<>4<>5<>6<>7<>8<>9<>10
Mad Scale	1<>2<>3<>4<>5<>6<>7<>8<>9<>10

I bet we could put all of our emotions into scales like this, but I want to only use these four for the discussion.

During an average day we would have different values for each scale at different times of the day, and the values would change with different experiences throughout the day as well. In my conversation with the insurance company my scales probably looked something like this:

Happy Scale	1<>2<>3<>4<>5<>**X** <>7<>8<>9<>10
Sad Scale	**X** <>2 <>3<>4<>5<>6<>7<>8<>9<>10
Depressed Scale	**X** <>2 <>3<>4<>5<>6<>7<>8<>9<>10
Mad Scale	1<>2<>3<>4<>**X** <>6<>7<>8<>9<>10

I wasn't depressed or sad, I was certainly mad but not out of control, and I was generally happy that day but not overly happy. Later on, when I made the realization that I wasn't happy, the scales probably looked like this:

Happy Scale	1<>2<>3<> **X**<>5<>6<>7<>8<>9<>10
Sad Scale	**X** <>2<>3<>4<>5<>6<>7<>8<>9<>10
Depressed Scale	**X** <>2<>3<>4<>5<>6<>7<>8<>9<>10
Mad Scale	1<> **X**<>3<>4<>5<>6<>7<>8<>9<>10

I wasn't sad or depressed, maybe just a little mad; after all, I yelled at my windshield because a car didn't let me in to the lane I wanted to get into and made me wait 5 seconds. I guess that made me a little mad, but I wasn't very happy either. I was kind of blah.

I feel, and I get to make this up because I thought it up, that anywhere from 1-3 on the scale of happy is kind of blah. Anything from 4-6 is generally happy, 7-8 is giddy, 9 would be bliss and 10 would be euphoria.

The sad scale would be: 1-3 not very sad, 4-6 generally sad, 7-9 maybe teary or crying, and 9-10 you would be crying hysterically, uncontrollable and bent over.

The depressed scale is: 1-3 not very depressed, 4-6 generally depressed with a little bit of unwillingness to do anything, 7-8 very depressed (not getting out of bed), and 9-10 you should be hospitalized.

The mad scale would again be 1-3 not very mad, 4-6 generally mad (raising your voice, maybe breaking a sweat), 7-8 would be very loud and scary, thinking about doing harm to someone, and 9-10 would be uncontrollable anger sort of like the comic book character The Hulk. "10 mad" is where things get broken and people get hurt.

If you think about this scale once again and imagine you can tune in your scale with knobs that control the scale, sort of radio-type control knobs, where would you like to tune yours to?

Happy Scale   1<>2<>3<>4<>5<>6<>7<>8<>9<>10

Sad Scale   1<>2<>3<>4<>5<>6<>7<>8<>9<>10

Depressed Scale   1<>2<>3<>4<>5<>6<>7<>8<>9<>10

Mad Scale   1<>2<>3<>4<>5<>6<>7<>8<>9<>10

I would think that most people would have the happiness scale at about 7-8 and the other scales down low at 1 or 2. I personally don't like bliss and euphoria all the time, although it is nice now and then, so that is why I think 7-8 is just great. If you want to win an argument maybe you would turn the mad scale up to about 6 to accentuate your point, but no one wants to be mad enough to harm someone unless that person is harming you or someone you love. Then I would turn it up to ten and maybe break the knob trying to go higher. I think the sad scale should be used appropriately to show remorse or sympathy, and try to stay away from the depressed scale if possible, unless you need to turn it down.

The reading on the scale would equate to the knobs looking something like this:

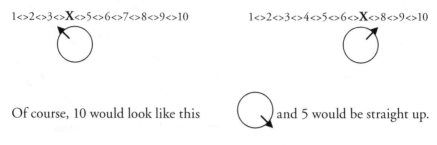

1<>2<>3<>**X**<>5<>6<>7<>8<>9<>10   1<>2<>3<>4<>5<>6<>**X**<>8<>9<>10

Of course, 10 would look like this   and 5 would be straight up.

Now that you have the fantasy of being able to control these emotions, you may actually find that you really can control them with your thoughts. Try it. When you're sad, try to imagine the sad knob and turn it down. If you are depressed or mad, try to turn that down as well. If you want to be happier, then turn that knob up. If you practice this, it will actually start to work over time and with practice.

I want you to understand that these knobs may not react to the scale immediately. The knobs have a sort of time delay, something like when you open the Internet on a slow computer. You click the icon for your browser and slowly the browser opens. Then the data starts to flow in and the text appears. Then the pictures start to form and fill in. Then finally you have your open page. Your emotion knobs will also react slowly at times. Just like pushing the button several times for a slow elevator, you may want to turn the knobs several times in your mind until you get the desired results.

I have called these knobs the "attitude adjustment" knobs. I am sure you have heard the expressions "you need an attitude adjustment" or "change your attitude"; well, now you can. By using the attitude adjustment knobs you will find that you can be happier if you desire and less sad if you desire that as well.

I would imagine that if you are depressed or mad it will be difficult to muster up the thought of the knobs, but you must try it. If you practice with the easiest attitude control knob, "happy," you will find that the others will become easier in time. Practice this exercise now. Imagine the four knobs:

Happy   Sad   Depression   Mad

Now circle on the scale where you believe you are right now:

Happy Scale	1<>2<>3<>4<>5<>6<>7<>8<>9<>10
Sad Scale	1<>2<>3<>4<>5<>6<>7<>8<>9<>10
Depressed Scale	1<>2<>3<>4<>5<>6<>7<>8<>9<>10
Mad Scale	1<>2<>3<>4<>5<>6<>7<>8<>9<>10

Now try to change your attitude settings. Picture yourself turning the happy knob up to about 7 or 8. Can you feel your mood changing? Turn down the others if they are high. Think about the knobs and the settings for at least 1 minute. Close your eyes if you have to, but concentrate on each knob individually and make a change in at least one of the scales. When the minute is up, chart your scale again and see if you have made a difference.

Happy Scale	1<>2<>3<>4<>5<>6<>7<>8<>9<>10
Sad Scale	1<>2<>3<>4<>5<>6<>7<>8<>9<>10
Depressed Scale	1<>2<>3<>4<>5<>6<>7<>8<>9<>10
Mad Scale	1<>2<>3<>4<>5<>6<>7<>8<>9<>10

Try this exercise at different times of the day and see if you can make yourself change the scale in different situations. You may even want to print out multiple copies of the scale, which can also be found at the book website www.25milliondollarmasterminds.com, and keep them with you for a week. Chart your progress and see if you can make a difference. Eventually you can add a scale and knob for just about anything you want to change in your life. Some examples could be confidence, faith, stress, willpower, and others, all of which will work the same as the examples above.

With this is mind, is it possible to give someone else an "attitude adjustment"? Wouldn't it be nice if we could just lift the access panel on our friends', co-workers', or spouses' backs and turn the knobs to make them more pleasant or less sad? Imagine that! If your spouse was mad at you, you would just say, "Turn around and let me you give an 'attitude adjustment.'" If your friend was depressed, you would turn her knob for depression lower and her knob for happy higher.

I remember a movie in which the premise was that a chemical spilled into either the air or the water (I can't remember which, but it is unimportant). The people in the movie, which took place in a large metropolitan city, had a strange reaction to the chemical. All of the people in the city were happy and nice to each other as a result of this chemical spill. The movie went on and it accentuated how great the world would be if everyone was happy and nice. A few people who were not affected felt that the production of society was being hampered so they came up with a cure to make the people normal again. Well, almost all of the people. Some could not be cured and they walked around happy and content and friendly forever. It was a 60's movie and probably had an agenda, but it made me think about how we actually have grown into a society that wants us all to conform—but that again is another book. But wouldn't it be nice if we were all happy all the time and pleasant to each other?

It is true that we can't turn the attitude adjustment knobs for our friends and family. If they haven't yet practiced this process, they may not be able to do it themselves either, but we can change the attitudes of others by how we react to their attitudes.

The first process in this is simply awareness. You must be aware of your friend's or spouse's current emotions. Are their knobs turned up or turned down? If they aren't happy, then make them happy. Most people try the approach of saying, "Come on, be happy already," or "Smile, it will make you happy," and quite often that not only doesn't work, it irritates the person you are trying to make happy and ends up irritating you as well.

Next time try to imitate the behavior you are trying to get them to do. For example, if you want to make someone smile, you would smile; if you want to make someone laugh, you would laugh. Something you have to remember is: to turn up the attitude adjustment knobs on someone else, take a lot of over-compensation on your imitation. I said a mouthful so let me simplify it for you.

You may need to laugh to get someone to simply smile and you may need to crack yourself up to get them to laugh. Have you heard the expression "laughter is contagious"? Well, it truly works. Action instead of words is the cure for the other person's attitude control knobs being set improperly. Finally, nice gestures can go a long way to making others happy. Sometimes just asking, "What can I do for you?" or "What can I get you?" will make all the difference. If someone has their "nasty" attitude control knob (one we haven't mentioned) turned up, then you can react in one of two ways. You can get nasty also, or you can try kindness. I suggest kindness if it is someone you care about. It really does work.

I remember one night, Carol, my girlfriend, was just in a bad mood. I had realized I hadn't done anything, but she was a firecracker waiting for the fuse to be lit. We had a discussion on who was going to pick up the cat's medication the next day, and because of family coming in and other crazy things happening the next day, it was hard for me to commit to saying I would pick it up. I could tell the sparks were beginning to try to light the fuse. We ended the discussion unresolved and I am sure she was even closer to exploding. We sat on the couch and barely spoke; the tension was building, but we still enjoyed a television show.   She said two words: "I'm hungry". Of course, I had already eaten and it was late.

Here come the choices: I could say, "There is food in the kitchen, go get something," or something like "I'm not hungry," but instead I said, "What do you want to eat?" She said sushi. It was 8 o'clock at night and I was in my PJ's. I said, "Okay, I will go get you sushi." I went out and brought back the sushi. Guess what happened next; she gave me a big hug and said, "This is why I love you, you are so good to me." She had a big smile on for the rest of the night and her happy "attitude adjustment" knob was now set properly.

If you are mindful of your own attitude settings and of someone else's settings, then you will realize you have the power to set these settings. Then you should expect to be in the state of "happiness."

Yes, true happiness does come from within, and money truly can't buy you happiness, but never use this as an excuse for not having money. Money does not bring misery either. Your attitude controls will decide your happiness or misery levels with or without money. Happiness and money are completely separate items and one should not cause the other to change.

With that being said, although I will be happy poor, I want to be happy and rich, so please read my next set of lottery numbers.

Remember to read them out loud.

4 11 13 33 47 Powerball 11

Chapter 15

Destiny

In the time it took to write this book, the stock market has reached what many believe is the bottom of about 6200 points and rebounded to over 10,000. Unemployment has risen to about 9.7% but is rising at a slower pace. The world is beginning to see the signs of the end of the recession. Some people are thrilled at this thought and believe their troubles are behind them. That is exactly what will cause you and me to forget the lessons we have learned and return to pending disaster.

Many news reports are saying that the American people are starting to spend money again. That means that the people who were starting to save money and actually hold onto money for an emergency are beginning to feel that the "candy bowl full of money" is filling up again. They are starting to buy items that they need and some that they don't need. At the time of writing this chapter, the government just finished an automobile rebate program that gave people a $4500 credit toward the purchase of a new car if they traded in their old clunker car. This "Cash for Clunkers" program generated billions in auto sales and helped to start up the automobile industry again.

Of course, most of benefactors of the "Cash for Clunkers" program now have monthly car payments that they didn't have before. That means that many of these people now have to restructure their budgets because the government gave them rebate money that was *burning a hole in their pockets*. They now have to work an extra few hours a day or week to pay that car payment. If they had read this book, maybe they would have thought twice about the purchase of a new car so soon after the height of this great recession.

This is why this book is timeless. Do not be fooled into thinking that you do not have to worry about how you should control and form your life after the recession is gone. Just like the recession came before, it will come again.

You must be prepared, through discipline, to make sure that it never happens to you again. The rest of the country may be crying the blues during the next downturn, but you and I will be safe and secure because we followed the rules laid out in this book.

The government of the United States is often blamed for the downfall of the economy. They are currently trying to initiate a government-run health care program because so many people are without health insurance. The people of the country want the government to take care of them just like a mother hen takes care of her baby chicks.

The blame for our problems does not lie with the government. The blame lies with each and every one of us. We must grow up and not be baby chicks. It is great that the government has social programs to help those in need, but only we can help ourselves to break out of the mold of mediocrity. This means that we must be prepared to take care of ourselves, regardless of what our country leaders decide to do or not do for us. If we had followed the rules outlined in this book for the last 10 or 20 years, then we would be like "the others" as described in chapter 6. These people can afford anything they need, including health care insurance. I am not against the government helping the needy; however, I am against being one of the needy that the government is helping. I suggest you adopt this philosophy as well.

This book described several ways to take your destiny into your own hands. You have the power to put money aside for retirement, for investment, for the right opportunity. You have the power to make your pursuit of happiness a joyous pursuit. You have the power to control all that you want in your life. As you have learned, you must clearly identify these needs and form a clear picture in your mind each day of what you desire and how you plan to get there.

The exercises in chapters 7 and 8 should have already helped you to discover your desires. Your fear/desire number line should have helped you realize some of the fears and excuses that you need to overcome to reach these goals. Your happiness "attitude adjustment" control knobs are now or will soon be in your control. You also realize that you need to increase your income sources and try to reach that goal of 7 income sources. You have learned various ways to maximize your wages income and you know that wages are always temporary. You have learned that it is the "passive incomes" that will truly make you rich and successful. You may or may not have already started a plan to make all of these things a reality in your life. If you haven't then I am sure you are contemplating them, and then you will either act or begin to act on these thoughts. The last thing to discuss is the killer of all dreams, and that killer is distractions.

Distractions from your goals will rob you of the opportunities that will present themselves. You must stay focused on your goal, and if a distraction interrupts your plans then you must continue your plans as soon as possible. Another warning is not to be fooled into thinking that a distraction is a goal. Be careful of these types of distractions. A good moral compass and strong belief in yourself and faith in GOD will help you avoid these distractions.

If you don't believe in GOD then you may have an empty hole in your spiritual being that may not be able to be filled. Some say that every person has a GOD-shaped hole in his or her heart that can only be filled with the spirit of GOD. This does not mean you cannot be rich and happy without GOD; it just may mean that you will not be filled with all you need. Either way, you will find that the Ten Commandments passed down to Moses on Mount Sinai make sense, not just on a Biblical level but on a level of how the human body and mind was constructed. It is a warning bulletin of items to avoid in order to make you a successful human. If you follow these commandments you will truly find fewer *distractions* keeping you from the success and happiness you desire.

Just like the clichés of money that were presented to you in chapters 2 and 3, I will use the Ten Commandments as rules to follow to ensure your success in life and in riches. Of course, I didn't write them; this is just a reminder that they apply to real life, not just for a lesson in Sunday School. I will attempt to make them non-secular and help to apply them in a non-religious way as well, but if you are a believer then you know the source from which they were written and should keep that Holy.

Here are the Ten Commandments as listed in the New King James Bible:

The Ten Commandments *(Exodus 20:2-17 NKJV)*

1   *"I am the Lord your God, who brought you out of the land of Egypt, out of the house of bondage. You shall have no other gods before Me.*

2   *"You shall not make for yourself a carved image, or any likeness of anything that is in heaven above, or that is in the earth beneath, or that is in the water under the earth; you shall not bow down to them nor serve them. For I, the Lord your God, am a jealous God, visiting the iniquity of the fathers on the children to the third and fourth generations of those who hate Me, but showing mercy to thousands, to those who love Me and keep My Commandments.*

3   *"You shall not take the name of the Lord your God in vain, for the Lord will not hold him guiltless who takes His name in vain.*

4   *"Remember the Sabbath day, to keep it holy. Six days you shall labor and do all your work, but the seventh day is the Sabbath of the Lord your God. In it you shall do no work: you, nor your son, nor your daughter, nor your male servant, nor your female servant, nor your cattle, nor your stranger who is within your gates. For in six days the Lord made the heavens and the earth, the sea, and all that is in them, and rested the seventh day. Therefore the Lord blessed the Sabbath day and hallowed it.*

5   *"Honor your father and your mother, that your days may be long upon the land which the Lord your God is giving you.*

6   *"You shall not murder.*

7   *"You shall not commit adultery.*

8   *"You shall not steal.*

9   *"You shall not bear false witness against your neighbor.*

10   *"You shall not covet your neighbor's house; you shall not covet your neighbor's wife, nor his male servant, nor his female servant, nor his ox, nor his donkey, nor anything that is your neighbor's."*

Commandment I

I am the Lord your God. You shall have no other gods before Me.

I find this one a little difficult to explain non-secularly or non-religiously; however, let's continue. We truly all have a spiritual hole that needs to be filled in our lives. As stated before, GOD fills this hole for his believers. The problem with believers and non-believers is what they choose as the most desirable of desires. If you wrote out your desires and they become reality, be cautious that they do not become your form of a god; this is truly the path to disaster.

Many of us became so obsessed with our successes and our egos in the past century that we, in a sense, made our egos and successes our god. No one should ever place themselves or their success in front of GOD. Even if you have not found your path to GOD you can clearly see that an empty hole that should be placed with the Spirit of GOD cannot be replaced with anything else.

You will often find happy, successful people who will state that their priorities in life are always faith, family, friends, and then everything else. For those of you who have not yet made the connection, that means that income or money, or sources of money, can only be as high as fourth on the list of your priorities in life.   Don't let the distraction of other gods get in the way of your success and happiness. Make sure your priorities are clearly defined and followed.

Commandment II

> *"You shall not make for yourself a carved image, or any likeness of anything that is in heaven above, or that is in the earth beneath."*

This commandment can also be interpreted as not worshiping false idols. This commandment orders us to not create an image or another likeness of false gods to worship.

A look back over the past two decades will clearly show you that we as Americans have created several false idols to worship. We have created the false idol of the big house, the false idol of the fancy car, the false idol of the big screen TV, the false idol of the second home, and so many others. We, in a sense, worshipped these things, and look where it has put this country today. We are now looking for the next false idol to worship and lean on. Give up the false idols and remember that worship belongs only with the Lord and not with the material things our money has created. If you are not a follower of GOD, then make sure that you do not worship anything. The only advice I can give you is that there is more to life than the things you are worshipping. Don't let these false idols get in your way and become a distraction from the important things in life.

Commandment III

> *"You shall not take the name of the Lord your God in vain."*

There are so many factors that control our successes and failures in life. Some of them appear to be out of our control. These may be illness, a car accident, or some other unforeseen tragedy that either stops us or slows our progress toward happiness and success.

Other factors are clearly in our control: our education, our drive, our commitments, and our disciplines in life. This is clearly what this commandment refers to. The definition of *vain* in this commandment in translated simply as "without significance." Making a promise to someone "in vain" would be to make that promise without any intention of following through with the promise. The Commandment states that if we want to follow GOD then we should promise to keep his Commandments, and our behaviors should praise and please GOD.

If you are not a believer, or have trouble with knowing what GOD wants our behavior to be, then you should be listening to not only your own moral compass but paying attention to how others perceive you. Your behavior should be that of a pleasing behavior to everyone around you. (By the way, I in no way mean that you should try to please everyone. I simply mean that we should control our behaviors to be pleasing to those around us.)

A great example of this is how we speak in public. Did you ever go into a restaurant and the people at the next table are very loud in their conversation? You came into this restaurant to enjoy a great meal. You ordered a special dish and you are enjoying it with the company of someone special. You are both aware of the conversation at the next table because, let's face it, they are rudely speaking well above the acceptable level in the room. You are tolerating it, but then it happens: someone, usually the big mouth at the table, decides to, very loudly, tell a dirty joke. The joke itself starts out distasteful, but the punch line has words in it that if his grandmother heard that kind of language she would wash his mouth out with soap. All of a sudden your great meal just doesn't taste all that great anymore.

Now think about all of the times that you have used unnecessary words and language in front of others. These are the behaviors that are subtly costing you years of success and happiness. To truly illustrate how our behavior affects us, think about some of these scenarios that may have happened to you or someone you have had contact with:

- A salesperson tells a dirty joke to a client; the client laughs, but somehow another company gets the sale.
- A man takes a woman out for a first date and flirts with the waitress. Although it was meaningless, the woman never returns the would-be suitor's calls.
- A father tells his son's wife that she is very sexy looking. The father wonders why his son hardly comes to visit.
- A teenager goes to meet his new girlfriend's parents for the first time. He uses foul language. He wonders why his girlfriend's father wants her to have nothing to do with him.
- A would-be employee tells a racial joke at an interview. The interviewer laughs but hires someone else.
- A politician who had an affair is perfect for the job of Mayor. The township votes the other guy into office.

Can you think of examples in life of this poor behavior that may have caused a negative outcome? When someone makes a commitment to live in GOD's life, they want to be sure that they please Him. The assumption is that GOD is always listening and watching your behavior.

So many of us do not realize that the people we come into contact with every day may already have an interpersonal relationship with GOD, or maybe just have a different moral compass than ours. We need to respect their views even if we are not a believer.

Acting Godly will always be the appropriate behavior in front of everyone, Godly or not, whereas acting ungodly will probably insult someone, Godly or not, in almost all situations. The best way to act Godly is to be aware that GOD is everywhere and He sees and hears all. This means that taking the Lord's name in vain, by behaving ungodly, may or may not always offend someone but it will always offend GOD. Another way to look at it is you never know who is listening. Why take the chance of acting ungodly, when acting Godly is very easy and pleasing to everyone?

This advice is for believers and non-believers. The effect it will have will greatly influence the quality of your success in happiness, business, personal relationships, and friendships. Don't make taking the Lord's name in vain, by acting ungodly, a distraction to your success and happiness.

Commandment IV

"Remember the Sabbath day, to keep it holy. Six days you shall labor and do all your work, but the seventh day is the Sabbath of the Lord your God. In it you shall do no work."

This is a great commandment for the tired and weary to understand. In this Commandment, GOD reminds us that we need to rest. Have you ever known someone who worked 7 days a week for a long period of time? I assure you that their level of happiness is very low and their level of energy is even lower. They cannot be happy if they do not take the time to sit back and enjoy a beautiful day to rejuvenate themselves.

GOD commanded the Sabbath to be a day of rest and reflection. Rest will help restore your energy and give you a new motivation to start the next day. Reflection is also an important part of the Sabbath. For the believer, the Sabbath is a day of reflection of all of the events GOD has helped to form over the past 6 days and before.

For the non-believer, a day of reflection is needed for all the things that happened during the past week and before that. Either way, it is important to reflect back on the good and bad in our lives. With this reflection we can make the minor adjustments in our life to help us achieve our goals and desires.

Think about a boat on the ocean. Let's say the captain sets a course for Hawaii from California. He simply points the bow of the boat toward Hawaii and never makes another course correction. With no other course correction, he will clearly be lost at sea forever. The captain needs to correct his course due to wind changes and water current changes on a regular basis. This analogy suggests that we need to make course corrections in our lives. One day a week is clearly the minimum amount of time we should use to correct our course. The reflection of the past week on this day will help suggest the course correction we need in order to succeed in both our personal and professional lives.

The seventh day of rest, the Sabbath, should be used for rejuvenation and reflection. This will truly help keep the distractions of a tired body and a miscalculated course from keeping us from our goals.

Commandment V

Honor your father and your mother, that your days may be long upon the land.

This Commandment should act as a reminder of the wisdom of our parents and the elders in our society. I remember a friend of mine who would often say, "The older I get, the dumber I get." This saying simply stated that he had realized that he did not and could not know everything about everything. Do you remember when you were a teenager and you knew "everything"?

In this Commandant, GOD reminds you that your mother and father are sources of great wisdom. They also do not know everything about everything, but I assure you that they know a lot about the areas in life you are struggling with.

If you respect your parents' knowledge and understand that their discipline or advice is from experience, you may learn something. With that knowledge you may avoid a great disappointment, heartache, or disaster in your life. When you were a child, your mother told you to stay away from the hot stove. She knew, just like you now know, that you would get burnt. The child who listens to their parent does not get burnt. The child who does not listen may have a scar for the rest of their life.

This may be a simplistic view of why you should heed the advice of your parents, but take a moment to think of the many times your parents gave you advice and you thought you knew better. Instead you got burnt or scared. Maybe they were right. If they weren't right, was the advice at least helpful to the situation? I think, if you truly listen to your heart, you will find that the advice was helpful most of the time.

Respect is another way to honor thy mother and father. Respect for your parents and caring for your parents will help you avoid guilt when they pass away. I remember my mother when her father died. My mother and my grandfather had little respect for each other and they hardly spoke in last 10 years of his life. I also did not speak with him in an effort to please my mother and because, frankly, he truly wasn't a very respectable person.

The day my mother received a phone call that he had died, she called me. She didn't sound very upset and told me not to even bother to go the funeral, and I didn't. You would think that she hardly would shed a tear for this man after the way their relationship deteriorated. After all, she told her son, his grandson, not to bother to go to his funeral. Could you have predicted that she was hysterically crying at his funeral? All of the things that she should or could have done, or should or could have said, could no longer be done or said.

She often feels the guilt of not honoring him when he was still alive, and now it is too late. This kind of guilt is the kind of guilt that takes years of therapy to overcome. Take the advice of the Father of all. Take the advice of GOD and honor thy mother, father, and the elders in your life and your days shall truly be long and happy. Don't have the distraction of guilt of not honoring your mother or father to hold you back from your desires and goals. Remember, their wisdom may lead you to your goals and desires faster.

Commandment VI

"You shall not murder."

This is a very simple commandment to understand and to understand why if you violate it, you will be unsuccessful and unhappy. I can't make this any clearer. Murder ruins so many lives, especially and including the murderer's life.

If you murder, one of two scenarios will transpire. The first is that you will get caught and go to jail, or be executed by penalty of death. There are very few successful and happy people in jail, and if you are executed that will obviously keep you from happiness in this life.

The second scenario is that you will not get caught and carry the guilt of the murder with you at all times. The guilt will clearly be a distraction and keep you from your goals and your success. Imagine looking over your shoulder every day for the rest of your life, thinking that the person you are sitting next to knows what you have done. Day after day the fear and guilt will eat at you.

There are so many stories that I have found about murderers ruining the lives of others and their own lives. I have decided not to tell stories of those who committed murder and how their lives were changed because I feel you can come to your own conclusions of how this can ruin you. Also, I do not want to sensationalize them. Murder is truly a distraction that you cannot recover from, ever!

Commandment VII

"You shall not commit adultery."

The best definition of adultery I have ever heard came from a 10-year-old child. I was assisting a teacher in Sunday School and the topic was the Ten Commandments.

The teacher would ask the children the definition of each commandment and what it meant to them. When he came to this one about adultery, I thought that none of the children in the class room could understand it at the ages of 9, 10, and 11 years old. I was truly surprised at the response of this 10-year-old girl. She said, "It is when you are dating someone or married to someone and you want to date someone else."

This is truly the definition of adultery. It is lusting for another person when you are in a committed relationship, or worse, when you are married. Adultery will ruin your chances of success and happiness until you stop it. Society defines adultery in many ways.

Adultery can be engaging in sexual activity with someone besides your wife; adultery can be engaging in an emotional relationship with someone of the opposite sex who is not your wife; adultery can be flirting with someone at a bar with no intention of actually pursuing a relationship with that person but is leading in that direction. It can even be looking across the room at a beautiful man or woman and thinking about being with that person, either emotionally or sexually. All of these are definitions of adultery and there are many more.

These acts of adultery will cause you to be severely distracted from your goals of success and happiness. I read once that a man who is very frugal and often cries poverty to his family will find an unlimited source of funds to spend on his mistress. This clearly is unacceptable behavior and will make it very hard to stick to the rules of 10% of your income to savings. This will make your success of saving for your retirement or an emergency greatly compromised.

Success in business will also be greatly compromised if you commit adultery. If you are using your energy to think of ways to see your mistress, you are taking precious brain power away from your business or your creation of the seven forms of income. There is no clearer example of this than a recent event of the governor of South Carolina. Governor Sanford ruined his carrier because of his adulterous relationship.

As with most adulterers, he put his mistress in front of his family, friends, and career. His mistress either became first over GOD on his list of priorities, or at best second on his list of priorities, thus ruining his career and his happiness. He thought about her and how to see her more than he thought about his family and career.

After a difficult day at the office the governor actually flew out of the country to meet her and told no one where he was going. Because of this misguided action, the governor has been asked to step down. He is in the middle of a divorce and his chance for a run for the presidency has been stopped dead. His divorce will cost him several thousands, maybe several hundreds of thousands, of dollars. His relationships with his children and the respect of his friends have been compromised forever. He truly will have a difficult time rebuilding all of the things that he worked so hard for.

Many people use the excuse of being unhappy with their current spouse to commit adultery. They claim that they are not happy with something or several things with their relationship. They then look for happiness in someone else. If this is truly the solution, then why do most people who cheat on their spouse end up not marrying the mistress? It is because the unhappiness came from within the person, the person who is the adulterer. They should have instead taken the time to adjust the "attitude adjustment" control knobs in their life to make themselves happy.

A final thought on this matter is that you cannot possibly have the energy to work on your marriage or committed relationship if you are taking some or all of your energy and using it to please someone else. I assure you that the act of committing adultery is causing problems in your relationship and your success in business, even if your partner or anyone else never finds out. If you truly want a successful life and truly want to be happy, then be faithful to your partner.

If your relationship truly needs to end, then let it end without it being tarnished with adultery. If you do not lust after someone else during your relationship and not even during the end of a relationship, you will be proud to know that you truly did all you could to save your marriage. Don't let adultery be the distraction that causes your failures in happiness and success.

Commandment VIII

"You shall not steal."

This one can simply be explained by rereading the description of commandment VI, *"You shall not murder,"* again. The reasons are basically the same: jail or guilt. The difference is that you may have a second chance after a few years of rehabilitation in a prison.

Another thing to think about with this Commandment is that we as humans can only truly appreciate things in life that we have earned or worked for. Stealing is a way of acquiring things or money without a proper effort to apply our talents. You may argue that a master thief is someone who has become a master at the art of thievery, so his theft will be justified and worked for. All I can say is, reread the story of Bernard Madoff in the cliché rule of "blood money" in chapter 3. Bernard Madoff was truly a master thief and now is a poor inmate in jail.

Stealing will catch up to you in several ways. Don't rob yourself of your desires with the distraction of stealing, especially when you can use that energy to better your life with more positive inspirations.

Commandment IX

"You shall not bear false witness against your neighbor."

The literal formation of the commandment means not to lie as a witness in court. If you are asked to give a testimony in a court of law, you are required to "tell the truth, the whole truth, and nothing but the truth." However it is believed in this Commandment that to "bear false witness" simply means to "lie." In this commandment you are simply told not to "lie" to others (neighbors).

Lying can cause you harm in many ways. Credibility in business dealings can be the difference between success and failure. If you must lie to make your product or your service appear better, then the odds are you will fail. How long do you think you can continue to lie before someone figures it out? Telling the truth will bring you credibility and success.

If you lie to family members and friends, your credibility will also be comprised. I once heard an expression that went something like, "You need to have a good memory to be a good liar." Lies have a way of tangling within other lies as well as tangling within the truth. How can you truly be happy if you constantly have to stop and think about what you have said in the past to people who think they can trust you?

It is much easier to tell the truth and be free of the lies and the confusion they create. Don't let lying, in your personal affairs as well your business affairs, be the distraction that keeps you from your success and happiness. If you think you can keep your lies from damaging your success, then you are indeed bearing false witness to yourself.

Commandment X

You shall not covet your neighbor's house; you shall not covet your neighbor's wife, nor his male servant, nor his female servant, nor his ox, nor his donkey, nor anything that is your neighbor's."

The last 20 years is a clear example of why this Commandment is so important. To *covet* means to want to possess something that belongs to another. It is clear that jealousy and greed is what brought the United States to its financial knees in the past few years. The greed of wanting to own a bigger house, or fancier car, or have more money, just because someone else had it, is what made people spend well above their means and had them make poor financial decisions.

Instead of being jealous of your neighbor's accomplishments, you should praise your neighbor, friend, or acquaintance that has worked for these accomplishments. If you are jealous of a person and want their lifestyle, then you cannot be open to the possibilities of that person sharing ideas with you. These ideas may allow you to learn how to have that lifestyle. You can learn so much from the people who have earned their way to success.

Many people in this country believe that it is unfair for successful people to have "all that money." "Why don't they give some to the poor", they often ask. What they are really asking is, "Why don't I have that money?" They ask this because they feel they deserve that kind of money, or at least a part of it. It is often the people without money who covet other people's money. These are also the people who believe the government should be responsible for their well-being. As I said before, I am all for helping those who truly need a handout, but I will not covet the money that others have; I will work for it instead. These people who want the handout usually believe that if someone is giving money away then they want to be first in line, so that they can take the most that they can before it runs out. These people are so busy coveting the money of others that they truly cannot devote any energy to trying to be one of the independent and possibly wealthy people.

The people who have riches usually have it because they deserved it. They earned it by working hard and doing the things that bring people up in this society. They did it by following many of the steps outlined in this book.

They didn't do it by being jealous or angry with others who have made a life for themselves. Instead they admired successful people and sought out the ideas that made those people rich and happy.

By coveting, your jealousy and greed will keep you from the true meaning of life. It will keep you from the things that will make others covet the things in your life. Covet nothing and you will have everything you need.

That is the review of the Ten Commandments and how, if you choose to follow them, you will have fewer distractions to keep you from your success. If you believe in GOD then you understand that they were written from the wisest of the wise. If you are not a believer then I hope you understand the wisdom of the Commandments and how they can truly make your life better. Following the Commandments will allow you to focus more on the important things in life and help you achieve true happiness and success.

Before I finish this chapter, I want to mention another serious distraction that may keep you from happiness and success. This distraction is addiction. There are many types of addictions, such as alcoholism, drug dependencies, sexual addictions, codependency, gambling, smoking, risky behaviors, the internet, and many, many more.

Addictions will keep you from your happiness and success almost always. Many people who have addictions may not be aware of the addiction or may not be aware of the ways the addiction is keeping them from success. Clearly someone who is addicted to anything is putting that addiction in front of everything.

If we refer back to the Ten Commandments, you should have concluded that breaking just one Commandment will make success and happiness difficult. Addicts are often breaking most or all of the Commandments. They break Commandments 1 and 2 because they put the addiction before anything and they make the addiction their god and false idol. They are clearly not adhering to Commandment 3 by not acting Godly. The very nature of the addiction (e.g., taking drugs, drinking alcohol in excess, gambling, etc.) is not pleasing to God. It is doubtful that an addict will take a break from anything on the 7th day. They certainly will not take a break from their addiction, therefore breaking Commandment 4. I have never heard of an addict whose mother and father approved of their addiction, so I would say they are not honoring them as Commandment 5 directs them to. Although not all addicts break Commandment 6 by murdering someone, there are several stories about addicts needing a fix so badly that they consider and sometimes commit murder for it. Adultery, Commandment 7, is another Commandment they may or may not break, but people will do anything for a "fix" when they are addicted. If adultery is the path to feed the addiction, then it is likely they will break this Commandment. Stealing is very common with addicts. They steal, breaking Commandment 8, simply to pay for or to steal the item they are addicted to. It is said that when you have an addict living in your house, make sure you hide your valuables. Commandment 9 is also broken often by addicts. They are always lying about their addiction and whether they are using or not using. Finally Commandment 10 says not to covet. Addicts clearly covet the things they are addicted to. If the addict has a neighbor with something they need, the addict will covet it and usually find it.

As you can see, it is impossible to have the success and happiness you desire with all of those Commandments being broken. If you feel you are a sufferer of addiction, be sure to find the appropriate help to overcome the addiction. The addiction, if allowed to run its course, will overcome your life and you will lose all control over your happiness and success. If you know someone who is addicted, then do your best to support them and help them break that addiction. To break the addiction you can try several methods, such as twelve step programs, addiction recovery programs, hospitals or other medical facilities. Search for what is best for you or your loved ones.

I have given you what I believe to be the foundation of all the tools you need to move forward into the world of money, hope, and happiness. By now you should be reading your affirmations, and following your budget. You should have a clear picture of where you want to go and how to get there. If not, then go back and reread the chapters that will help you define these things. Start using the tools in this book to make your desired world a reality.

You have a great opportunity to move up in life and make a difference. It is the destiny of both you and me to be admired, respected, happy, healthy, and wealthy. It is also our destiny to pass this knowledge on to others so that they can open their eyes to the path to their destinies as well. **It is our destiny to win, or *metaphorically* win, $25,000,000 in the lottery!**

Now for my final set of lottery numbers.

4 10 15 32 52 Powerball 11

Remember to read…
…never mind, the money is already starting to accumulate and I have already found my hope and happiness.

I hope you have found yours as well.

May God bless you in your pursuit of all your dreams and desires!

Appendix

Lottery Numbers in the book

Powerball number

15	27	30	32	53	11
5	21	24	40	44	11
14	25	29	43	48	11
12	22	32	42	52	11
11	15	30	42	48	11
14	21	23	25	41	11
12	13	14	22	31	11
12	14	25	31	41	11
18	23	30	34	49	11
14	22	24	32	41	11
2	6	12	14	33	11
4	5	9	10	25	11
9	14	26	29	39	11
4	11	13	33	47	11
4	10	15	32	52	11

Powerball is a registered **trademark** of the Multi-State Lottery Association

Bibliography

Chapter 5

1   "The History of the Lottery." *The History of the Lottery* (2006). *Winning With Numbers*. Web. <www.winningwithnumbers.com>.

2   "How likely am I to hit the jackpot in the Mega Millions lottery - and how do the odds compare with being hit and killed by lightning?" *Dr. Knowledge*. Ed. John Swain. The Boston Globe. Web. <www. boston.com>.

3   Goodstein, Ellen. "8 lottery winners who lost their millions." *MSN Money*. Bankrate.com. Web. <www.moneycentrel.msn.com>.

4   Witt, April. "Rich Man, Poor Man." *The Washington Post*. 2005. Web. <www.washingtonpost.com>.

Chapter 6

1.   "Lottery winner claims simplicity is key to happy life." Lottery winner claims simplicity is key to happy life (2007). Lottery Post. Web. <www.lotterypost.com>.

2.   Floiran Kratz, Ellen. "Taking Home the Jackpot." Taking home the jackpot (2007). CNN Money.com. Web. <www.money.cnn.com>.

Chapter 7

1.   Osteen, Joel. "Sermon entitled Persistence and Determination." *Inspired Growth*. Web. </www.inspiredgrowth.net>.

2.   Hill, Napoleon Think and Grow Rich "Law of Autosuggestion" chapter 4 Ballantine Books New York 1937

Chapter 9

1.   www.brainyquote.com.   Web.   <http://www.brainyquote.com/ quotes>.

Chapter 12

2.   IRS Code, Section 61.

Chapter 14

1.   "Quotations about Life." *The Quota Garden*. Web. <www. quotegarden.com>.

2.   Leonhardt, David. *The Happy Guy,* Web. <www.thehappyguy. com>.

MLM companies mentioned in this book are copyrights and trademarks of their respective corporations.

Suggested Reading List

"Think and Grow Rich" by Napoleon Hill
"The Secret" by Rhonda Byrne
"The Power of Intention" by Dr. Wayne Dwyer
"Awaken the Sleeping Giant Within" by Tony Robbins
"The 100 Absolutely Unbreakable Laws of Success" by Brian Tracy
"The Richest Man in Babylon" by George S. Clason
"Rich Dad, Poor Dad" by Robert T. Kiyosaki
"The Pearl" by John Steinbeck
"The Millionaire Next Door" by Thomas J. Stanley

Websites for review
www.focusmyhealth.com/millionaires
www.lotterypost.com
www.profundraisers.com

Official website for the book
www.25milliondollarmasterminds.com
At this site you will find several of the worksheets and other helpful ideas discussed in this book.